Stuart Library
of Western America

UNIVERSITY OF
THE PACIFIC

WITHDRAWN

Modelling the Golden Hinde

Frontispiece: *Arthur L Tucker's completed model of the Golden Hinde.*

Modelling the Golden Hinde

Editor Arthur L Tucker
Deputy editor John Bowen
Art editor Jon Blackmore
Editorial assistant Stephen Morrison

MODEL SHIPWRIGHT
GREENWICH

© 1973 Model Shipwright

LIBRARY

JUN 1 6 1976

UNIVERSITY OF THE PACIFIC

313998

Published by
Conway Maritime Press Limited,
7 Nelson Road, Greenwich, London SE10
ISBN 0 85177 078 9

Western
Americana

VM
142
M68

Front cover
The Golden Hinde by E J H Gardiner
Back cover
Sir Francis Draeck (Picture by courtesy of the
National Portrait Gallery, London)

Set by Jaset
Printed in Great Britain by Whitstable Litho,
Straker Brothers Ltd.

Contents

Preface

A number of years ago the urge to build a ship model came over me. Unfortunately at that time, there were very few books or other related sources available that would be of help to the beginner and I was at a loss to know where to start.

I visited the Science Museum, South Kensington, London and was inspired by the wonderful collection on display. Most of the models were contemporary but a few were modern, notably the *Cutty Sark* built by Dr C Nepean Longridge, the rigged model of an English ship of about 1426 by A C Jackson, the rigged model of an English Man-of-War by R Morton Nance and the rigged model of an Elizabethan Galleon of about 1600, made in the workshops of the Museum.

I had a long talk with Mr Fricker, who was then rigger, and he kindly let me copy out some tables of mast and spar dimensions which I believe came from a manuscript dated 1611, preserved in the Pepysian Library at Magdalene College, Cambridge, England, and attributed to Matthew Baker. Later I managed to obtain photographs of the elevation and sail plan of a four masted warship and also four sections of a ship of about 1586, both from a manuscript which Samuel Pepys had entitled *Fragments of Ancient English Shipwrightry* which is also in the Pepysian Library. In *Old Ship Figure-heads and Sterns* by L G Carr Laughton, I found a coloured reproduction (Plate 6) of *An Elizabethan Galleon: probably the 'Ark Royal'*, (From *Ancient English Shipwrightry*, Pepsyian manuscript, Magdalene College, Cambridge, England).

From all this, and using the proportion of three breadths = length and a good deal of guess work, my model was born. It is not a scale model of the *Golden Hinde* as nothing is known about her size or appearance, but it is a pleasing model to make and, when finished, it looks fairly seaworthy and decorative. It differs in appearance from the full size replica recently built at Appledore, possibly because different lines of research were followed although as far as I am aware, the Matthew Baker manuscript is the only original work of such an early date in existence.

I have endeavoured to write an account of how to build the model in a way that the novice making a first attempt will be able to follow without difficulty. It should be possible to build the entire model from raw material; I did not use one single bought part when I made mine. As to the length of time it will take, this depends entirely upon the speed at which one works and also the amount of detail one is prepared to include.

Brief historical notes have been included as it is felt that a knowledge of Drake and his epic voyage round the world will stimulate interest in the project. Richard Hakluyt's account of Drake's circumnavigation has been preferred to all others, partly because of its contemporaneity and factual reliance, and partly for its engaging narrative prose style. Together with the historical notes, it is intended to furnish important related material which hitherto has proved troublesome to locate.

I wish to acknowledge the work of John Bowen in producing the plans of the model and also the detailed sketches which appear throughout the description. But for his skill, co-operation and encouragement, this monograph would never have been written.   *Arthur L Tucker 1973*

ACKNOWLEDGEMENTS

We should like to thank the following for their help in the production of this book:

A C Littlejohns AMPA, Bideford; Bodleian Library, Oxford; British Museum, London; Colin Duffield; Douglas Allen Photography, Somerset; Gordon Knight of Mulberry Marketing and Merchandising Company Limited, UK representatives of Golden Hinde Limited of California; National Maritime Museum, London; National Portrait Gallery, London; Pepysian Library, Magdalene College, Cambridge; Popperfoto, London; Science Museum, London; Waverley Photographic, Barnstaple.

Historical notes

by Stephen Morrison

The *Golden Hinde* first appears in historical records under the date of 15 November 1577, as the *Pelican*. On that day, with four other vessels, she slipped out of Plymouth harbour on a voyage which was destined to bring her and her captain great fame and wealth. It was, as Richard Hakluyt (1552?–1616) tells us, the beginning of Francis Drake's circumnavigation of the World. The three year endeavour, recounted by Hakluyt and set out below, yielded new lands, vast amounts of Spanish treasure and a reputation which ensured for the vessel a then unprecedented popularity for more than eighty years.

For Drake too, the rewards were considerable, but he was shrewd enough to entertain the possibility of incurring the displeasure of powerful enemies at court during his absence. Accordingly, on 20 August 1578, as he entered the Strait of Magellan, he caused the *Pelican* to become the *Golden Hinde,* in honour of Sir Christopher Hatton who, shortly before Drake's departure from England had become a favourite of Queen Elizabeth. Sir Christopher's crest was a 'hinde trippant or'.

There is no evidence to suggest whether Drake's motives were well-founded or not, yet his reception on his return in December 1580 was as unequivocal as he could have desired. By express command of the Queen, an elaborate walled enclosure was constructed at Deptford Dock to accommodate the ship which stood as a memorial to the daring and enterprise of her captain. On a royal visit to the dock, during which the Queen dined in the ship's cabin, Master Drake was knighted; the delight and enthusiasm of the crowd on that day is vividly portrayed by William Camden, the Elizabethan antiquarian and historian, who observes that, 'there was such a concourse of people, that the wooden bridge over which they passed broke, and upwards of a hundred persons fell into the river, by which accident, however, there was nobody hurt, as if, he says, that ship had been built under some lucky constellation'. (quoted by Dews *History of Deptford*).

Such impassioned fascination may have been partly engendered by the appearance of the royal person, but the continued presence of the eager-eyed London populace testifies to the considerable popularity which the ship enjoyed, the cabin of which, it appears, was converted into a refreshment parlour.

The events surrounding the ultimate fate of the *Golden Hinde* are a good deal clearer than those relating to its inception, the place and date of which are, to this day, unknown. It is certain, however, that the ship ended its life in the dock at Deptford some time before 1662.

Exposed to both the elements and the buzzing multitude, the ship fell into disrepair, decayed and was finally broken up. The Master Shipwright of the dockyard, Mr John Davis, mindful of the need for some memorial to remain, had a chair and a table constructed from some of its timbers. The chair, which was presented to the Bodleian Library in Oxford, bears a dated

Left: A line engraving of Francis Drake executed by Robert White (1645–1704), the English engraver and draughtsman. Measuring 10.1/8" by 7.1/8" in its oval frame, it is one of the plates in Harris' 'Collection of Voyages' (1705) in the British Museum, London. (Picture by courtesy of Popperfoto)

11

inscription of 1662; the table now rests in the Middle Temple in London, and is the one from which Sir Francis Chichester dined after being welcomed back from his single-handed circumnavigation of the world.

'A very large and strongly-built ship of several hundred lasts, exceedingly fit to undertake so protracted and dangerous a voyage, and well able to bear much buffeting. The cabins and armouries [were] in fine order as in a well-built castle, the middle where the largest cannon are placed being eighteen good paces wide'. The words belong to Frederick, Duke of Wurtemburg who, in 1592, visited the dockyard and left this fine but brief impression of the *Golden Hinde's* construction and sea-worthiness. Research has uncovered a good deal more reliable information on this.

Leaving aside for the moment the question of the tonnage and the dimensions of the vessel, it is certain that the *Golden Hinde* was a sheathed ship, and was double-ceiled. Her upper deck (the main deck) was of hatches and not planked. In all, she had five decks: the lower or gun deck, the main deck, the half deck, the quarter deck and the poop deck. It is estimated that there were two cabins at the stern, the 'Great Cabin' on the main deck, and 'Drake's Cabin', immediately above on the half deck.

Of the eighteen guns she is known to have carried, seven heavy guns were carried in each broadside, and the bows were fitted with the remaining four.

Douglas Bell, in his *Elizabethan Seamen,* states that two flags flew from her masts. The ensign of St George, the flag of England, flew at the main mast, and aft was the Tudor flag, comprising horizontal green stripes quartered with a St George's Cross.

Estimates as to her complement vary from source to source, as well as, more credibly, from voyage to voyage. Hakluyt, at the beginning of his account states that 'with a fleete of five ships and barques, and to the number of 164. men, gentlemen and sailors', the small convoy set off. The *Golden Hinde* herself, it seems, was capable of carrying, in the words of Douglas Bell, 'ninety men or more, officers, seamen, boys, musicians and tradesmen such as smiths, carpenters and coopers'. This figure may be taken as being the maximum, with 71 or 72 as the minimum, although on one voyage the figure had apparently dropped to 59. Since no definite authentic figure exists, it would be unwise to pursue this point any further, and totally unsatisfactory to use these figures in an attempt to gauge the dimensions of the ship.

This outstanding problem of dimensions and tonnage, the most difficult and enigmatic question mark which hovers over the *Golden Hinde*, has been the subject of much discussion and theory for many years. Certain tentative conclusions have been reached, notably by Dr Anderson and Mr Naish, both of whom were, for a long time, associated with the National Maritime Museum. Here, in a slightly condensed form, is a summary of their findings.

Dr Anderson's research centres on the recorded estimate for docking and enclosing the *Golden Hinde* at Deptford in 1581. Clearly, if the measurements of the enclosure are known, it is possible to gauge the probable limits of the vessel. The document, now in the British Museum, gives details of the proposed work, the most important of which are a brick wall to contain in circuit 180' in length, with a width of 24' to leave room for a path.

From this he estimates that the wall, including the sides and ends was 180' in length. The ends were 24' each, so the sides could only have been 66' at the most. The ship for which the wall was built could, therefore, have the following dimensions: keel 40′, beam 16′ and depth (probably less than half the beam) about 7′. Using the formula:

$$\frac{\text{Keel x beam x depth}}{100} + \frac{1}{3}$$

the tons and tonnage would only be 60. This figure seems to be too small, and contradicts most sources which state that the *Golden Hinde* was of 100 tons or thereabouts.

The ambiguity of the wording of the estimate leads Dr Anderson to search for another alternative, since the first figure obtained is not satisfactory. For him, the most plausible solution is to assume that the wall was open at

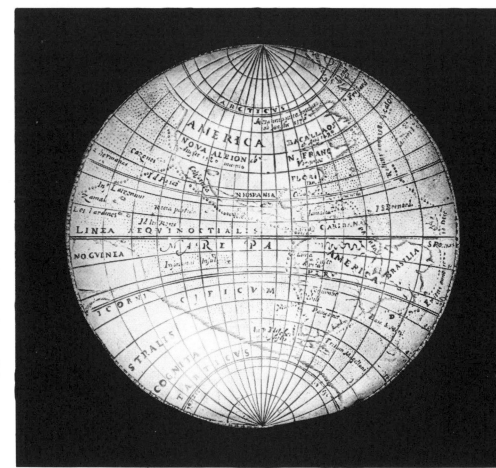

The Drake Silver Map. A cartographical representation of the Western and Eastern Hemispheres engraved on the two sides of a silver medallion 68mm in diameter.

Of the nine copies known to exist, one bears the name Michael Mercator and the date 1598. It is said that Drake, while on a secret mission for the Queen in the Netherlands in October 1586, commissioned Michael Mercator to draw him a map of the world, showing the track of his circumnavigation voyage. At the same time, he ordered a miniature of this map to be engraved on a silver medal

The map is of considerable cartographic importance; it is very exact and completely up to date, depicting not only the newly-established colony of Virginia, but also the Drake discoveries in Upper California. The course taken by Drake on his voyage round the world is marked with a dotted line. (Picture, larger than actual size is by courtesy of the National Maritime Museum, London).

one end, even though this breaks the 'circuit'. In this case, the length of each side would be 78'. The ship would then be 67' from stem to sternpost with a keel of 47', a beam of 19' and a depth of 9'. She would measure 80 tons and her tons and tonnage might be as much as 107.

Apart from this obscurely worded estimate, there are several conflicting statements as to the tonnage of the ship. In 'The World Encompassed', compiled by Francis Drake's nephew and namesake, the *Golden Hinde* is said to have a tonnage of 100. Hakluyt, in his account below, says that she was of 120 tons and a record in a state paper refers to the *Pelican* as being of 150 tons.

These discrepancies are the subject of perhaps the most comprehensive article written on this problem by Mr Prideaux Naish. In it he asserts that

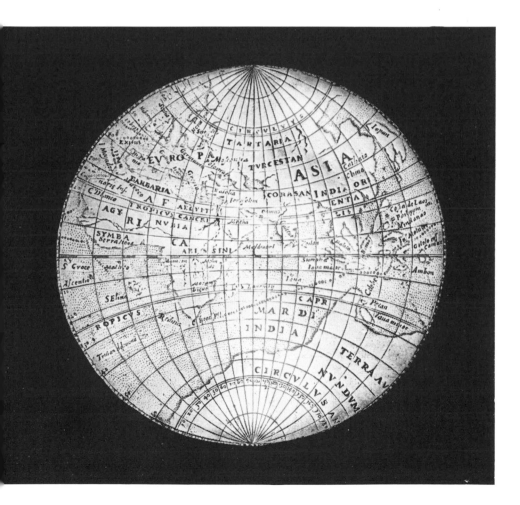

the figures of 100, 120 and 150 may all be correct as regards the tons and tonnage of the *Golden Hinde*. He resolves this apparent mathematical contradiction by pointing out that, before 1581, tonnage measurement was calculated in many different ways, and that no standard formula was evolved until some time later. The general formula, he states, was to multiply the length of the keel by the beam, and the result by the depth. This, referred to as the 'solid number', was divided by 94 or 100. The result was the ship's burden in tons. By adding 1/3 or 1/4 of the number to the number, the ship's tons and tonnage was ascertained.

He demonstrates the arbitrariness of the system by declaring that the keel was measured with or without the False Post; that the beam was measured inside or outside the planking, but the wale was never included. In addition, the depth of the hold could be defined as from the top of the keel to the main deck, or from the ceiling to the beam; alternatively, the measurement might be the draught of water when the ship was fully laden. Therefore, according to which variation was chosen, the tons and tonnage of the *Golden Hinde* was 100, 120 and 150.

Mr Naish concludes by affirming that Dr Anderson's findings are plausible, although he can see no reason why the wall at Deptford should not have had semi-circular ends. Granted this, his estimate of the dimensions of the vessel seem to coincide well with those of Dr Anderson, and he agrees that a ship of such dimensions could have been installed in the dock with ease.

This summary attempts no definitive solution to the question of the dimensions and tonnage. The highly factual articles referred to, however, go a long way to resolve the inconsistencies and establish an argument of no small validity.

Bibliography. Douglas Bell *Elizabethan Seamen,* Longmans 1936; Nathan Dews *History of Deptford* Revised 1884, Conway Maritime Press 1971; F C Prideaux Naish *The Mystery of the Tonnage and Dimensions of the 'Golden Hind,'* Mariner's Mirror Volume XXXIV 1948; R C Anderson *The 'Golden Hind' at Deptford,* Mariner's Mirror Volume XXVII 1941.

A representative model

by Arthur L Tucker, with drawings by John Bowen

Tools &
Materials

Tools. The tools required to make a model of this kind are few and not expensive to buy. The first essential is a chisel about 3/4" or 1" wide, and of good quality, as it will be used a great deal when carving the hull; one having bevelled edges and known as a 'paring' chisel is preferable to the heavier type 'firmer' chisels. A small but good quality oilstone, having one side smooth and the other side coarse, is necessary for keeping edge tools sharp; sharp tools make the work easier, and blunt tools can be dangerous. A chisel, when new, is ground to an angle of 25°, so it will have to be sharpened to an angle of 35° before it can be used. Never try to sharpen any tool on a dry oilstone; use a few drops of thin oil and be sure to wipe the stone clean after use, and keep it in a box to protect it from dirt and dust. For those who are unsure of their ability to sharpen their own tools, the inexpensive 'Eclipse' honing guide Number 36 is a great help.

Next in order of priority is a 'coping' saw; this is a useful tool for cutting curves and shaping thick pieces of wood. It will save a lot of work when making the hull of the model, if used to cut away the surplus wood before starting to carve. The important thing to remember is to keep the blade taut by means of the adjusting screw, and thus lessen the chance of the blade breaking; spare blades are usually sold in packets of ten, and are quite reasonably priced.

It is possible to work without a vice on this model, but it is very much better to have one to hold the work and act as a third hand when necessary. One having jaws about 2.1/4" wide and opening up to 2.1/4" is quite large enough for any job which the model shipwright is likely to tackle.

Another tool which, although not essential, is most useful for shaping such items as the hull block is a spokeshave. These are made either of metal or

Left: The completed model (All pictures except for the Rope spinning jenny, page 48 by Arthur L Tucker)

19

of wood; it is easier to get a fine adjustment on the former type. In use, the tool is held in both hands and if the blade is finely set it can be used to remove shavings as thin as cigarette paper, even from a curved surface. A tip worth remembering is that the merest smear of oil on the sole of the tool will help it to slide smoothly over the wood, but it is essential not to apply the oil too liberally otherwise it will soak into the wood and be most difficult to paint afterwards.

Certain parts of the model have to be cut from very thin plywood, and the best tool to use for this job is a fretsaw (known in America as a jigsaw) though if one is not available, such cutting can be done with a craft knife, or even with a very sharp penknife. The centre member of the model is 1/4" thick and this is much more easily dealt with by a fretsaw or, failing that, by a coping saw used with care.

Two or three needle files are essential for cleaning up gunports and other openings in the model, the most useful types being a 'round', a 'three-square', a 'hand', and a 'knife', all about 6" long. It is worth getting a file handle, as this will protect the hands.

It will be necessary to buy a small pin chuck or even two, one about 3" long with a capacity of 0" to 0.04" and one slightly larger with a capacity of 0.03" to 0.062", together with a packet of darning needles and a packet of assorted needles. The method of using the needles is to break off the eye at

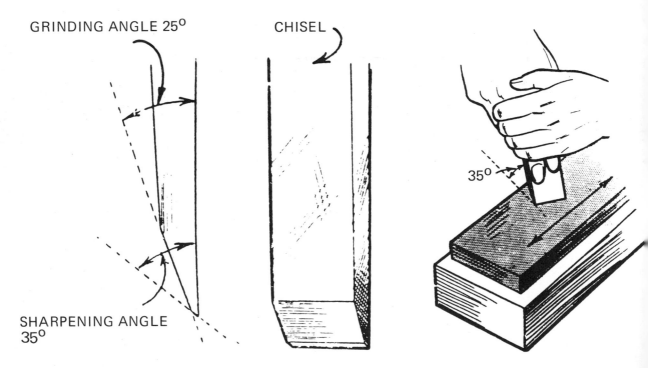

GRINDING ANGLE 25°

CHISEL

SHARPENING ANGLE 35°

35°

the point where it joins the needle (this is slightly thicker and forms a shoulder), and then sharpen the broken end to a diamond point on the side of the oilstone, not forgetting to use a little oil. The sharpened needle, when held in a pin chuck and twisted, will pierce wood and thin metal with ease.

Another useful tool is a pair of side-cutting pliers, mainly used for cutting wire, nails and pins. If the points of small nails are cut off before driving them in, there will be far less likelihood of splitting the wood, especially if it is thin. The addition of a pair of round nosed pliers to the kit will greatly increase the range of fittings that it is possible to make. A small lightweight hammer of the kind known as a 'pin' or 'telephone' hammer with a head weighing 4 ounces is also useful for the model maker. The type known as ball pein has one head flat and the other domed, and can be used for shaping soft metal.

A single-pinion hand drill with a chuck capacity of 0–5/16″ can also be used as a makeshift lathe for turning up wooden gun barrels and similar objects. The wood should be rounded. This can be achieved by using short lengths of dowel. These are held in the chuck and shaped by filing while they are rotated by turning the drill handle. In this way, it is possible to turn out very reasonable gun barrels, capstans and other similar items quite quickly.

From left to right: Chisels should be ground to an angle of 25° and sharpened to an angle of 35°.
The correct way to hold a chisel when sharpening it.
The incorrect angle formed by 'rocking'
A wood or metal template for use in testing the grinding and sharpening angle of chisels, plane irons and spokeshave irons.
Method of removing the 'wire edge' from the back of edge tools after sharpening.

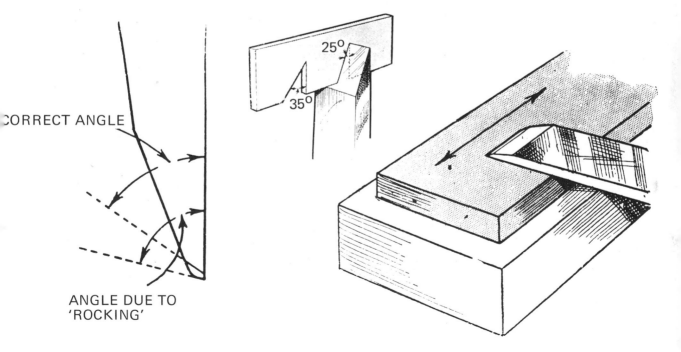

CORRECT ANGLE

ANGLE DUE TO 'ROCKING'

25°

35°

There is on the market a small, reasonably priced, plane known as the 'David', obtainable at most craft shops. This tool takes the thick type of razor blades and is most efficient in its performance. A few household clothes pegs with the ends sawn off and shaped will be found useful for holding parts while the glue is drying, as will the 'Bulldog' clips now available in many sizes. Another 'tool' which will be found invaluable for rigging, especially when belaying ropes, is a crochet hook.

Two pairs of brass tweezers are needed. Steel ones should be avoided as they can get magnetized and become a nuisance. One pair of tweezers should be adapted by cutting or filing about 1/2" off the points and leaving the ends square and approximately 3/8" wide. A semicircle should then be filed in each of these square ends and the ends should both be turned inwards to form a pair of claws. This tool will save much searching on the floor and many sore fingers, as it is used to hold rigging blocks, deadeyes and other small parts while glasspapering or filing them. The second pair of tweezers will be used for rigging when the time comes; they should be protected when stored by keeping the ends stuck in an old cork. In time the modeller relies so much on these tweezers that he feels very much handicapped if they are mislaid. A few sheets of glasspaper of different grades will complete the outfit:— three sheets of the finest grade, two sheets of medium grade and one of coarse grade, will do for a start. Care should be taken when using a very coarse glasspaper as it is inclined to make deep scratches in the wood, which can only be removed by a lot of hard rubbing. A useful

Right: Two sizes of pin chuck (top); these are used for holding small drills or sharpened needles and are operated by rotating between the thumb and fingers; they can also be gripped in the chuck of a lathe and will hold particularly fine work. A jeweller's small flat file, a 'rat tail' file, a knife edge needle file and a square 'precision' file (centre). A craft knife; this type is usually sold with spare blades which can be had in a variety of shapes (bottom).
Centre right: A hand fretsaw frame. This picture shows the two wing nuts used both for holding the blade and for adjusting the tension of it. With this tool the most intricate shapes can be cut out both in wood and metal
Far right: A coping saw. This tool will cut wood up to 1" thick and will easily follow curves. The blade is tensioned by rotating the wood handle.

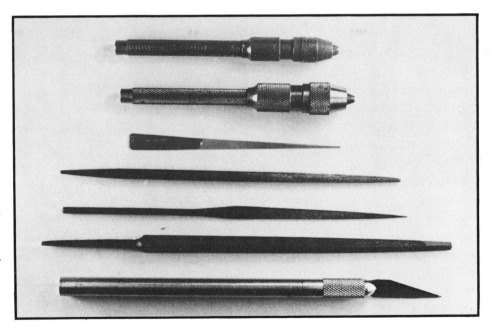

Top: A metal spokeshave showing the screw adjustment; also a wooden spokeshave which has the blade fixed and adjusted by screws.

Centre left. The correct way to sharpen the cutter of a wooden spokeshave.

Centre right: A small vice which can be clamped to the workbench and removed easily. An essential in every model shipwright's tool kit.

CUTTER OF WOODEN SPOKESHAVE

Top, left: *Two pairs of tweezers suitable for use when rigging, also a round or 'rat tail' file in a quick release handle.*

Top, centre: *'Bulldog' clips are available in many sizes and are just right for holding rails and other small parts in position while the glue is drying. Crochet hooks are also made in a variety of materials and sizes; they are most valuable for rigging as they will pick up a rope from across a crowded deck without doing any damage.*

Far right: *A small but invaluable plane which uses razor blades instead of an iron (top), also a small 'ball pein' hammer, the rounded head of which can be used for shaping thin metal*

Bottom, left: *Improvised lathe using a drill with its handle planed, to fit snugly in vice.*

Bottom, centre: *A pair of side cutters for general use in cutting wire, pins etc. With this tool, pins can be cut off close to the work and tapped home with a small hammer; it is particularly useful when fixing wales or planks to a hull. Round nosed pliers are used for shaping wire, making eyes in the ends of pins, wire rings and many other small items.*

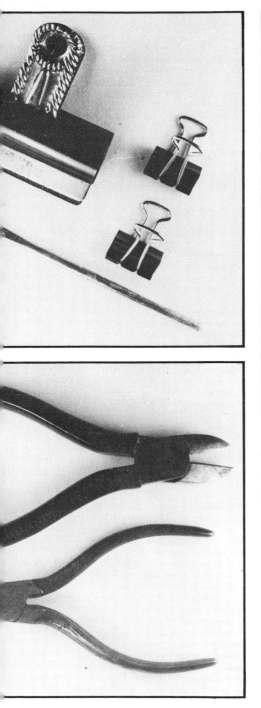

hint learnt from an old cabinet maker is to follow up the final sanding by giving the work a polish with the back of the glasspaper.

Glues and paint. For gluing the main members of the hull, a waterproof type of glue such as 'Cascamite' should be used, but in order to avoid trouble the manufacturer's instructions must be followed when mixing. It is inadvisable to use an impact type adhesive as once the part is in position on the job it is impossible to move it if a mistake has been made when placing it; with the other type there is ample time to slide the part back into its correct position. For the smaller parts such as deck fittings, decorative mouldings and so on, a liquid glue such as 'Seccotine' or Humbrol 'Britfix' clear adhesive Number 22, will be found more satisfactory since it does not have to be made up every time it is required.

It was the custom in Elizabethan times to decorate ships with bright colours rather than with the carved and gilded work used later. Humbrol paints are perhaps the best on the market, but flat paint should be used throughout rather than a gloss finish. Poster paints could also be used for all the brightly coloured decoration; they are known to have stood the test of time very well. It is better not to economise when buying brushes. Three—one each of fine, medium and large sizes—are all that are required. They must always be stored clean and with none of the bristles bent. If these simple precautions are taken they will last for many years.

It is essential to spend some time studying the plans, and getting the 'feel' of the model and a general idea of the shape of the hull before starting work. Time spent doing this is of very great help during the building of the model; it is never time wasted.

Building the Hull

Materials. The first problem to be faced in starting to make a model is, what timber to use for the hull. Yellow pine is undoubtedly the best for the purpose, but it is next to impossible to obtain it today. However, there are a number of good soft woods available such as lime, white pine, obechi and Oregon Pine (balsa wood is not suitable for this model as it is too soft). Rigging blocks, deadeyes and other small parts are best made of boxwood; this is also hard to obtain, but an old ruler made of this hard straight grained timber can be used for the purpose. Holly is another lovely white tight grained timber which is sometimes available.

Construction. The main construction consists of a centre member sandwiched between two large blocks of wood representing the hull proper, above which are smaller blocks to make up the forecastle, half deck, quarter deck and 'poop'. The centre member should be made from a piece of wood 25″ long by 7.3/4″ wide by 1/4″ thick. This can either be solid wood or plywood, but if solid wood is used the grain must run lengthwise. First, the outline is traced from the plan (figure 1); this is a silhouette of the hull and includes the keel, rudder, deck lines and figurehead. This must now be transferred to the wood by placing a sheet of carbon paper under the tracing (held firmly in place by drawing pins) and going over the outline with a hard pencil. Using a fretsaw or coping saw, cut round the outline keeping the cut just outside the pencil line, as this allows for any irregularities, especially on the keel and the deck outline. There is a rectangular slot in the bow which should be cut out at this point, either by sawing out with a fretsaw, or by drilling two or three small holes together in the waste wood and joining them up by means of a small file.

Wrap a piece of medium grade glasspaper round a block of wood about 4″

by 2″ by 1″ and clean up both sides of the piece, then finish off by using a fine grade glasspaper, polishing with the back of the paper. Care is essential at this stage that the edges do not become bevelled during the glasspapering. Suitably shaped files are used to sharpen up the outlines of the figurehead and rudder, and a plane is run along the keel to make sure that it is perfectly straight. With a craft knife or a very sharp penknife, a V groove is cut on each side where the rudder joins the hull; later on, straps to represent the hinges, or more correctly the 'gudgeons and pintles', will be fitted. The centre member is now complete except for the figurehead which will be dealt with later.

The body of the hull consists of two blocks of wood, each measuring 1′5.1/2″ long by 3″ wide by 3.9/16″ in depth. These can be of solid timber or can be built up of several layers to the required dimension. If several layers are used, they must fit together accurately and be glued under pressure using either cramps or weights.

On the deck plan there is a centre line running the length of the ship. Another line is now drawn parallel to, and 1/8″ away from this centre line on either side of it on the plan, to indicate the width (1/4″) of the centre member. A tracing of half, that is, one side of the deck outline, using the line just drawn as the centre line is now made, following the dotted lines from the bows (keeping to the outermost line on the drawing) right to the stern. After making sure that the hull blocks are absolutely square by checking them on all sides with a 'square' and correcting any discrepancy by planing, the thirteen station lines, shown as numbered vertical lines on the plan, are ruled right round each block using a square—this is a good test for

FIGURE 1
OUTLINE OF CENTRE MEMBER

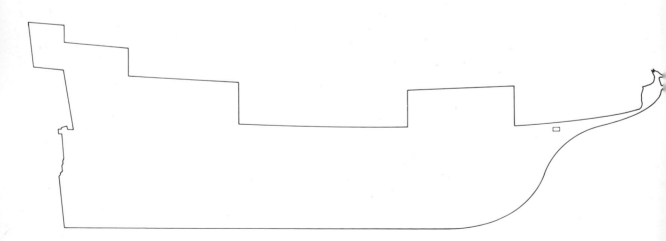

the accuracy of the hull blocks, for if they are quite square the lines will meet all round. It is important that these lines should not be lost during the shaping of the hull, and those which have been cut away during carving should be redrawn.

The tracing of the deck must be transferred to the narrower face of one of the hull blocks (figure 2), making sure that the (new) centre line coincides exactly with one edge of the block, and the outline of the deck is marked off as before, using carbon paper inserted between the tracing paper and the block. The tracing should be reversed and the other block marked out in the same way, thus making a right and a left hand block for the main part of the hull. Both blocks are now turned upside down, and the process repeated by drawing the deck outlines on the underside of each block. The outlines on the top and bottom of each block must coincide. The next job is to trace the side elevation of the hull blocks; this corresponds to the outline of the shaded area on the plan marked 'main hull blocks'. This outline is transferred to the sides of each of the main blocks, both back and front, checking that the tracing is facing the right way, that is, with the bow of side tracing to bow of deck tracing. The horizontal line on the plan at the top of the shaded area should be placed along the top edge of the block (figure 2).

Before starting to carve the blocks it will be necessary to make a set of templates from the body plan showing the shape of each section. A separate tracing of each of these sections is made from the plan (actually they are half sections and there is no need to do one for each side of the ship), and these are transferred on to stiff cardboard. Sections 1 to 6 are forward of the midship section, (which is Number 7) and those numbered 8 to 13 are aft of the midship section. A mark must be made on each template 3.9/16″ above the bottom to act as a datum point and the position of the centre line of the ship marked in. The best shape for the templates is shown in figure 3.

Begin by cutting along the deck line on the blocks with the coping saw, then remove the waste wood at the bows and stern to the outline (now only visible on the inside of the blocks). The resulting shape will be a fair indication of the final form of the hull after the surplus wood is carved away. A good method of holding the blocks while carving is to screw to the back of the block to be worked on a strip of wood a little longer than the hull and about 1″ by 1/2″ section. This can then be held in the vice at any angle, thus leaving both hands free. Model makers who have no coping saw can start shaping the blocks by first removing one bottom edge with a plane or spokeshave and then gradually shaping the hull, checking all the time with the templates as the work progresses. When finished, the two blocks have to be a matching pair, hence the necessity for the frequent use of the section templates. Each block will finish about 3/8″ narrower at the

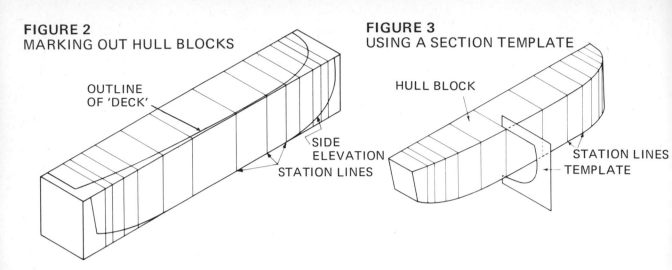

FIGURE 2
MARKING OUT HULL BLOCKS

OUTLINE
OF 'DECK'

SIDE
ELEVATION
STATION LINES

FIGURE 3
USING A SECTION TEMPLATE

HULL BLOCK

STATION LINES
TEMPLATE

top than at the waterline, due to the 'tumble home', (that is, the sides of the ship lean inwards).

When carving, the tools must be kept sharp by frequent stropping of the cutting edge of the chisels on a piece of leather. It is inadvisable to remove the wood in large chunks; it is better to take off thin shavings and gradually work down to the shape indicated by the templates. Carving should always be with the grain of the wood and not against it, and the modeller must remember the golden rules—never carve towards the hand, which should always be behind the chisel, and that blunt chisels are dangerous.

When both blocks are of the correct shape, they should be given a good rub down with medium grade glasspaper. Many blemishes show up at this stage, but irregularities can be given a touch with the chisel or spokeshave and another glasspapering with medium grade and then with a fine grade glasspaper, finishing off with a good polishing using the back of the glasspaper. The two main blocks can now be fitted to the centre member. The best way to do this is to drill and countersink two holes in the centre piece fairly well away from the edges and also drill two corresponding pilot holes in one of the blocks—having first made sure that the block is held in its correct position against the centre member. By putting some glue on the block, placing it in position against the centre piece, and driving two screws through the centre member into the pilot holes, the block is located accurately in place. Now the other block must be glued and carefully positioned against the other side of the centre member with as much pressure as possible applied while the glue is drying. 'Cascamite' glue is ideal for the job, providing the maker's instructions are followed. While applying pressure, the hull must be protected with a pad made of old rag, or even several thicknesses of paper, before applying the cramps, and the modeller must make sure that the block does not move out of position as the pressure is applied.

While waiting for the glue to dry the model maker can prepare two blocks for the forecastle each 4″ long by 3″ wide by 1.1/2″ thick, two blocks for the half deck each 6.1/2″ long by 2.3/4″ wide by 1.7/8″ thick, and two blocks for the quarter deck each 3.3/4″ long by 1.7/8″ wide by 1.3/4″ thick. The forecastle blocks are glued in place against the centre member, after cambering the tops of them to form the deck. Then the half deck blocks are shaped using the plan of the centre member as a guide; this deck is cambered and also slopes forward and the after end of these blocks has to slope to conform to the shape of the centre member.

Next comes the quarter deck and the poop, each being cambered and sloping forward. As these blocks overhang the sides of the model, the templates should be used for finishing as before. The main deck—that is, the top of the main hull lying between the after end of the forecastle block and the fore end of the half deck block—must also be cambered as shown on the

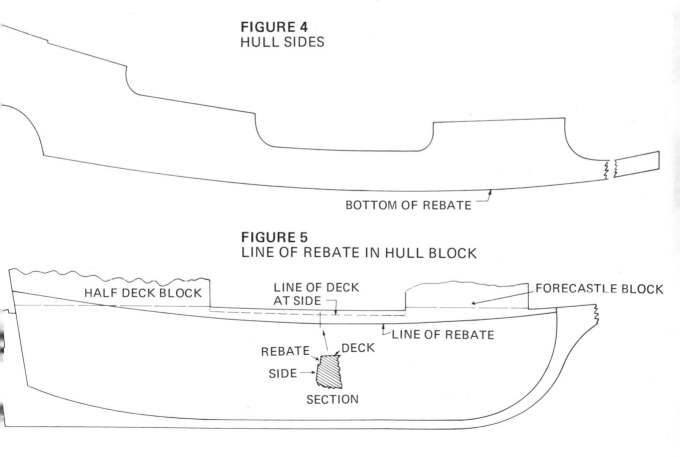

FIGURE 4
HULL SIDES

BOTTOM OF REBATE

FIGURE 5
LINE OF REBATE IN HULL BLOCK

HALF DECK BLOCK

LINE OF DECK
AT SIDE

FORECASTLE BLOCK

LINE OF REBATE

REBATE   DECK

SIDE

SECTION

plan. This can be done either before or after these two blocks are fitted. The holes for the masts and for the bowsprit can also be drilled at this stage. It will be necessary to support the hull firmly before doing so, and also to ensure that the masts are vertical to the hull when seen from forward or aft. The masts each have a slight rake aft when seen from the side, as is indicated on the plan, and the angle of the bowsprit must also be checked from the plan.

The next job is to make and fix the hull sides, which consist of two ply-wood shapes extending the whole length of the ship. They enclose the decks from the wale or rubbing strake below the gunports to the top of the gunwales of the decks, and at the forward end of the ship they enclose the beakhead right up to the figurehead. As these pieces have to follow the curve of the ship it is not possible to trace the whole of the shape from the flat plan, but it is not so difficult to get the correct shape as it may at first appear.

From the drawing of the centre member on the plan, a tracing should be made of the curved dotted line which extends from the bow to the stern just below the line of the main deck—this will be the shape of the lower edge of the hull sides. Two pieces of thin plywood 3/32" thick are needed, each about 26" long and 5.1/2" wide. The curve just traced should be transferred to the bottom edge of one piece of plywood. Along this curve the waste wood is cut away with a craft knife. A point to remember here is that the curved line just traced will start about 1.3/4" from the after end of the plywood (figure 4), and should be extended to both ends of the plywood, the reason for this being that the plywood has to reach to the extreme end of the poop deck.

After cutting along the curved line and cleaning up with glasspaper, the strip must be bent round the hull from stern to figurehead and temporarily pinned to the hull. The positions of the various decks are marked, and a pencil run along the bottom of the curve to mark the hull where the side will eventually be fixed. The strips are now removed and the top shape, gun ports, railings, and the openings at the beakhead are marked in from the plan. Although this shape must be taken from the plan, it will have to be modified slightly to compensate for the curvature of the hull. Both pieces

FIGURE 6
GUN PORT LIDS
AND HINGES

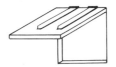

of plywood are pinned together, the shape cut out and the edges cleaned up with sandpaper. Before fixing these hull sides in position, the parts of the inside that are visible should be painted a matt red (post office red or Humbrol B R red Number 137). The curved line marked on each side of the hull should be carefully cut with a craft knife and then with a very sharp chisel a rebate in the hull blocks is cut to the depth of the plywood used for the hull sides (figure 5), so that when they are fixed in place they will lie flush with the main body of the hull.

At the bows the rebates run out where the hull sides leave the main hull and extend toward the figurehead. The sides must be glued firmly to the main hull, inserting a few pins for safety, the extreme ends which reach the figurehead can be held in place with rubber bands for the time being. When the glue on the hull sides is dry, the ends are joined in just behind the figurehead, and glued firmly to the centre member. A capping rail, as shown on the plan must not be forgotten. The body of the 'hinde' figurehead is built up of plastic wood as realistically as possible. This is coated when finished with a coat of gold paint (Humbrol metallic 16/97).

The gunports should now be cut in the hull. Their positions are marked off from the plan, and then a 3/8″ diameter hole is drilled in the centre of each; with a small chisel or a file these are opened up to 3/8″ square. Care must be taken to keep the sides of the openings square to the line of the keel. The ports for the guns on the main deck will have already been cut out when preparing the hull side pieces. All the gun ports except for those on the main deck have lids (figure 6) which are square and can be made from

Below: The beakhead, showing figurehead, belaying pin rail, cleat on the side of the bowsprit for belaying the spritsail yard halliard and leading blocks for the spritsail yard braces. In this photograph the forestay is shown passing through the forecastle. This is incorrect, and the lead of the forestay should be clear of the forecastle edge, as shown on the sail plan. Note also the second hawse hole on the port bow—this applies to the port side only.

scraps of plywood; they are hung on hinges which can be made from very thin brass shim, or even thin card.

Along the length of the hull on either side run the wales; these protect the hull sides and are represented by strips of timber about 1/8″ wide and 1/16″ thick. There are three wales in all, one about 1/2″ above the waterline amidships and running from just below the hawse hole in the bows to near the tiller at the stern, one running from just below the beakhead to the bottom of the quarter gallery at the stern, (note that there is a break in this wale where the main chainwale or channel which takes the rigging of the mainmast comes), and one running from the cathead right through to the curve just below the transom. These wales are glued and pinned into place, and care should be taken when bending them round the bows—it might be advisable to steam these to prevent them breaking under the strain.

Holes are drilled on either side of the bows to represent the hawse holes; these are the holes in the hull through which the anchor cables pass. The

Below: The stern gallery with arched supporting brackets; also the mizzen channel The rope shown attached to the ring bolt and returning to the hull is the main sheet.

catheads, which are used when weighing the anchor, are made from lengths of wood 1/4″ square set into holes cut into the hull. They are supported underneath by small wooden brackets. In the top of each cathead six small holes are drilled and each pair of holes is joined with a shallow groove (figure 7) to represent the sheaves.

In order to give the decks a neat appearance and to cover up the joins, false decks should be made from thin plywood. These must have the deck planking marked on them, which can be done with a 4H pencil, after which they should be given a coat or two of clear matt varnish and be glued firmly in place.

From the plan, a tracing is made of the transom, that is, the part bearing the coat of arms, and transferred to thin plywood. After cutting it out and making sure that it fits neatly and accurately in place on the model, it should be removed and painted in the correct colours, adding the coat of arms and the other decorations; then it is fitted and glued in place. It is much easier to do it this way than after it is on the hull.

The next items to be made and fitted in place are the channels, which are cut from wood 1/8″ thick and shaped as shown on the deck plan. Each one is cut to fit closely to the side of the hull and glued in place; as these have to take a considerable strain from the rigging, it will be as well to drill and pin them for added strength. The gunwales are fitted on their top edge with capping rails, as can be seen on the plan; these can be made from thin plywood, and should be glasspapered to a slightly convex section.

A piece of cardboard is used to make a template of the stern and quarter gallery; it is necessary to study the plans carefully in order to get the correct shape. When the modeller is satisfied that it fits accurately, the shape is transferred to thin plywood and cut out. The gallery has panelled rails all round and is supported by brackets, the shape of which are shown on the plans; it is also supported by three overhead arches on either side (figure 8).

FIGURE 7
CATHEADS

FIGURE 8
GALLERY ARCH PIECE

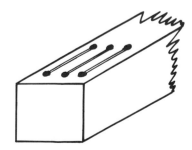

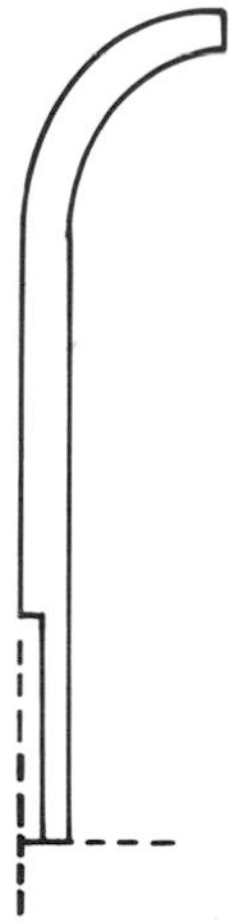

Deck Fittings

In the head of the ship just behind the figurehead is a triangular shaped grating. There are several ways of making this part. One is to file the point of a nail to a square section and then punch out regular lines of holes in a piece of thin plywood, or even cardboard, and then cut to shape. Another is to take thin narrow strips of wood and glue them on to thin paper, using one of these strips of wood as a spacing gauge. When a large enough area has been covered, a second set of strips is glued across the first at right angles. When the glue is dry, the paper foundation is gently removed with glasspaper and the grating cut to shape. Afterwards, this is fitted in place in the bows. It should be noted that a belaying pin rail is fitted across the beakhead; this takes the running rigging of the head sail.

The bulkheads numbered 15, 16, 17 on the plan are cut from thin plywood or from veneer. If using plywood, the deck rails are included and after the bulkhead is fixed in place, the rail uprights are reinforced with small pieces of wood. Then a capping rail is fitted on top to take the belaying pins. With a little care these bulkheads can be made to look very realistic by gluing on pieces of veneer to represent the doors, with pieces of thin dowel (glass-papered fairly flat) on either side of the doors for the half columns. The windows, or lights, are cut out as well and a slight recess made in the deck blocks behind the windows and painted black; a piece of cellophane is then glued to the back of the bulkhead in each window opening.

There are four sets of belaying pin rails to be fitted inside the bulwarks as shown on the plan; they should be made of thin wood and cut to shape. They must be securely fastened, as they have to take quite a strain from the rigging. The belaying pins can be short lengths of pin or wire pushed through holes drilled in the rails, leaving about 3/32" showing above and below the rail. The gratings on the forecastle and on the main deck can be made in the same way as described for the beakhead.

The bitts in front of the main and mizzen masts are just square posts sunk into holes in the deck. The tops of the posts are bevelled and a pin or piece of wire pushed through a previously drilled hole; these pins must run athwartships, that is from side to side, and should project about 1/4' on either side. The posts are painted the same red colour as used for the inside of the bulwarks (gunwales).

The deckhouse on the half deck can either be cut from the solid or, preferably, be built up from thin plywood, adding the doors and windows in the same way as on the bulkheads.

There are seven ladders to be made; these are constructed on a jig made from a piece of wood of the same width as the ladder (about 3/8") with a series of sloping saw cuts in it the distance apart of the stair treads (figure 9). Small pieces of card or veneer are then inserted in each saw cut and long

Below: The forecastle bulkhead viewed from the outboard end of the bowsprit showing the rail with belaying pins, deck grating and 'cat heads' on either side of the forecastle; these latter were used for drawing up the anchors into position for stowing.

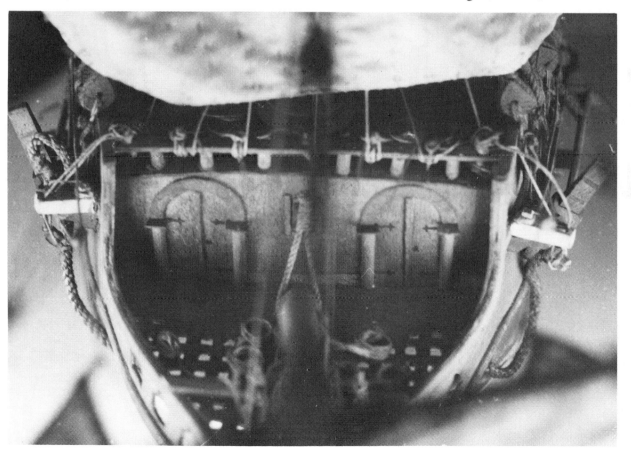

side-strips glued to the ends of these treads. If the jig is well rubbed with wax (a candle will do) before the treads are put in position, the glue on the side members will not adhere to it and the completed ladder will be easy to remove.

The guns are made from thin dowel rod which can either be shaped with a file while holding the rod in the hand, or the dowel can be held in the chuck of the single-pinion drill referred to in the section on tools; the drill is then fixed in the vice and used as a lathe with a hand-held file acting as the lathe 'tool'.

The gun carriages can be shaped out of a solid strip of wood about 3/8″ square. First, a piece the length of the carriage is cut off, and three saw cuts are made at the position of the three steps, each cut being slightly deeper towards the back of the carriage (figure 10); then, the cuts along the grain are made with a sharp craft knife. The gun carriage is finished off by making a groove along the top to take the gun barrel, using a round or 'rat tail'

Below: The main deck showing gratings, the bulkhead at the after end of the forecastle (on right of picture), On the left, the mizzen stay can be seen attached to the main mast, the woolдings (ropes wound round the mast to strengthen it) can also be seen on this mast.

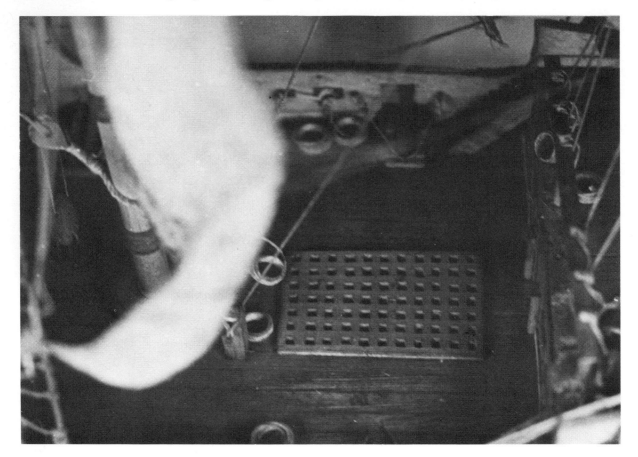

Left: The half-deck bulk-head and the lower part of the mizzen mast showing the special halliard block, also the deck house in which the 'whip staff' would have been housed in the period before the introduction of the steering wheel In the foreground is a swivel gun mounted on the gunwale.

file. The alternative method of making the carriage is to cut out the side shapes in pairs from thin plywood and glue them to a strip of wood of the correct width. The wheels, or 'trucks', can be made from card punchings. The correct colour for the guns at this period is bronze, and the carriages can either be painted matt black, or left as unvarnished wood. The swivel guns are made from very thin dowel (such as cocktail sticks), and thin pins; the swivels are made from bent wire.

FIGURE 9
JIG FOR MAKING LADDERS

FIGURE 10
GUN CARRIAGES

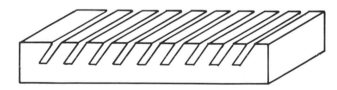

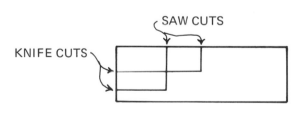

SAW CUTS

KNIFE CUTS

Painting the Hull

After making sure that the hull has been thoroughly glasspapered and that no blemishes or bumps remain, the first job is to mark in the waterline. The model must be stood squarely on its keel and be supported in place with some blocks of wood. With a pencil held on a block of wood of the correct height, the line of the waterline all round the hull is marked in. After masking tape has been applied to the hull above and along the waterline, the hull is painted below this waterline with a thin coat of flat (matt) white paint. The gunwale above the top wale where the decorative work is to come later, the transom and the rail around the quarter and stern gallery are painted white to give a good base on which to do the final painting. When the paint is quite dry it should be given a gentle rub down with well-used fine glasspaper.

The lower part of the hull can now be given a top coat of flat white or ivory oil paint. From the waterline up to the middle wale it is painted dark brown, and above this up to the top wale the wood should be left natural colour and given a coat of clear matt varnish. The space between the top wale and the deck rail at the forecastle and the space up to the level of the quarter deck at the after end (the part already given an undercoat of emulsion) should now be carefully marked out to receive the design.

To do this, a horizontal line should be drawn between the upper and lower edges, then the perpendicular lines, taking care to keep them evenly spaced, and, finally, the diagonal lines from top to bottom should be drawn. This is easier than it sounds if the details on the plan are followed carefully. The top row of triangles which have been formed should be painted green and red alternately and the lower row green and yellow. Above this, the space level with the quarter gallery is painted blue with the scroll work on it painted white; this design continues right round the stern in the same colours.

The transom is painted white and the Tudor coat of arms and four Tudor roses are in full colour. The lion is yellow, the dragon red, and the shield blue and red at the top and red and blue at the bottom quarters, with the details picked out in yellow. All the wales are painted dark blue right up to the figurehead. The panels on the quarter and stern gallery are alternately blue and yellow; those with the Tudor rose in the middle are yellow, and those with the fleur-de-lys are blue. The gunport lids are painted black on the outside and red on the inside.

One small job which should be done at this stage is to fit the dummy hinges to the rudder. These may be either strips of very thin copper or brass shim, or alternatively metallic faced paper could be used with good effect. If metal is used, it will be necessary to drill and pin it in position.

Masts & Spars

The best timber to use for these items is lancewood or degame; failing this, any really straight-grained softwood such as yellow or white pine will be satisfactory. It is better to start by splitting the wood down the grain rather than by sawing it as the parts will be much stronger when made in this way. Measurements for all the masts and spars are taken direct from the plan, but at least an extra inch must be allowed on the lower masts and the bowsprit for sinking into the hull. Having split off suitable lengths of timber slightly oversize for the job, the wood is planed into a square and then into an octagonal section; finally it is finished to a round section, first with coarse and then with fine glasspaper.

The masts taper and must be made thinner at the top than at the bottom, while the yards are thickest in the middle and taper towards either end. The flagpoles should also be made at this stage; the little round 'trucks' at the top of these and at the top of the mizzen are made from small beads of appropriate size. When finished, the masts and spars are given a couple of coats of clear matt varnish, rubbing down with fine glasspaper after the first coat. An alternative method of finishing the masts and spars and one which will not increase their girth is to paint on a coat or two of french polish and, when dry, give a dull finish with the back of a piece of glasspaper.

The deadeyes at the period of this model were heart-shaped and should only have one hole in the middle. The easiest way to make them is to obtain some plastic knitting needles of the right diameter and then file two flats on the rod to produce a pear-shaped section (figure 11). Then a fairly large hole in the end of the rod, about 1/8" deep, must be drilled. With the edge of a triangular file, make a groove round the rod as near to the end as possible. The deadeye is then parted off just below the groove. Eighty-six are needed in all and, if the prospect of making so many does not appeal, it is often possible to buy them already made from the better model supply shops.

A large number of rigging blocks are also required and the best material for making these is either boxwood, holly or even sycamore. First, strips of wood square in section are cut to the width of the finished block. A pencil line is drawn down the centre of each face, and the length of each block is marked off. A hole for the sheave is drilled and, by using a triangular file first on one side and then on the other, the block is parted off from the stick. The block is then finished by cutting a shallow groove on either side with a file and finished off with glasspaper (figure 11).

The circular platforms on the masts, known as 'tops', are quite a feature in sailing ships. There are several ways in which these can be made, the most simple being to cut out the base from fairly thick plywood, say 3/16″ thick, not forgetting to cut the four openings at the same time. Next, from a piece of wood about 1/2″ thick a ring is cut out with the same diameter as

FIGURE 11
RIGGING BLOCKS

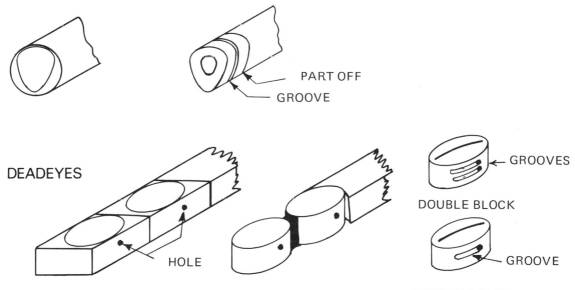

PART OFF

GROOVE

DEADEYES

HOLE

GROOVES

DOUBLE BLOCK

GROOVE

SINGLE BLOCK

the base, and another ring is cut to the outside diameter of the top from a thinner piece of plywood. These three rings are glued together, and the space between the top ring and the middle ring filled with plastic wood. It must be neatly worked to give a smooth and fair curve (figure 12). Of course, if these tops are turned on a lathe, it will make a neater job.

At this point it is advisable to make a stand for the model. This is a matter of individual taste; some people like to place the model on pillars and others prefer it on crutches. If the latter is preferred, the hull templates for sections 6 and 10 for the inside shape must be used, but the outside may be finished in any way which is desirable. Having decided on a shape, it is better to draw half of it on a piece of paper; then the paper is doubled along the centre and the outline cut out with scissors; thus, both sides are made alike.

The pattern is transferred to wood about 1/2″ thick, cut out and cleaned up with sandpaper, (figure 13). Two pieces of 3/8″ dowel rod long enough to hold the crutches apart at the appropriate distance are cut. Two 3/8″ holes are drilled in each crutch. The dowels are glued in place after cleaning them up with glasspaper and finally the whole stand should be given a coat of varnish.

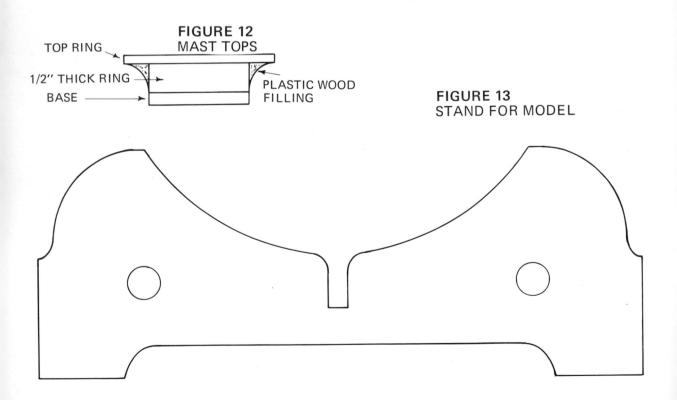

FIGURE 12
MAST TOPS

TOP RING
1/2″ THICK RING
BASE
PLASTIC WOOD
FILLING

FIGURE 13
STAND FOR MODEL

Rigging

As it is becoming increasingly hard to buy the various sizes of cord needed for rigging the model, the best way out of the difficulty is to make cord on a rope-making machine. This consists of three parts, as shown in the diagram. The part that does the spinning consists of three or four hooks operated by small cogwheels, which are turned by a handle attached to a larger cogwheel. The part of the machine holding the cogwheels should be held on the table by a clamp. The free running hook is usually mounted on a ball bearing and attached to a travelling stand, which can be weighted according to the size and strength of rope to be made. The third part is a boxwood 'top' shaped like a pear and having three or four grooves in its length, and inserted in it is a rod long enough to reach the board on which the work is being done. This is to prevent the 'top' from turning during the spinning operation.

To operate the machine, lengths of cotton are taken back and forth from the machine to the spinner according to the thickness of the rope to be made. The handle is then turned until a 'lay' appears in the twisted cotton. The 'top' is now inserted between the three (or four) lots of twisted strands at the end farthest away from the machine. The handle is now turned again until the 'top' starts to move up on its own, which it will continue to do until it reaches the machine. The cord should now be well stretched and cut off, when it will be found to keep its shape without trouble. As the end with the single hook moves up due to the cotton getting shorter as the turns are put into it, it should not be held fast but should be allowed to slide; however, it is necessary to put some weight on it to prevent it getting too slack. Too much weight will make the finished rope hard and not enough weight will make it soft.

Four stranded rope is seldom used in model making, three stranded laid up 'right handed' being the usual. For running rigging a lightish brown colour is used and for standing rigging a very dark brown or black.

It might be as well at this point to mention splicing, seizing, bends and hitches. The only two kinds of splices needed for this model are an eye splice and a cut splice. To make an eye splice, the end of the rope is unlaid for a short distance. An eye is formed of the desired size and the three ends are laid on the 'standing' part. The middle strand should be tucked through a strand of the standing part next to it, against the lay of the rope, then the strand on the left is passed over the strand under which the first strand is tucked and it is tucked under the next. The remaining strand is tucked under the third strand on the other side of the rope. Now each strand is again tucked alternately over a strand and under a strand of the rope. The ends are cut off and a little liquid glue is applied. The splice may be rolled between the fingers or between two small pieces of wood into a neat taper. To make a cut splice, the ends of two lengths of rope are unlaid and placed on a table in such a way that one end faces right and the other faces left, leaving enough space between to form an oblong loop. The ends of one rope are tucked into the strands of the other, as in an eye splice, this will leave a loop in the middle. A touch of glue is applied and the splices are rolled as before. A seizing is made by taking a number of turns around the two parts of the rope bringing the end through between the parts and taking a few more turns before tying off.

Below: The four stages of making an eye splice.
1. Unlay the end of the rope for a short distance, make an eye of the required size and tuck the middle strand of the unlaid part under any strand of the rope against the lay.
2. Take the left hand strand over the strand just tucked and under the next strand of the rope.
3. Take the last strand under the remaining strand on the other side of the rope.
4. Repeat the whole process tucking the ends under the alternate strands. Cut off the ends, smear with liquid glue and roll between the fingers to make a neat finish.

A reef knot, two half hitches and a clove hitch are the only knots which will be needed on this model.

Standing Rigging. This is the rigging which holds the masts firmly in place and, apart from adjustments due to stretch or other causes, it remains static. The first job is to fit the lower deadeyes to the channels—the narrow shelves which project from the sides of the ship opposite each mast. The necessary number of holes are drilled in each channel, as shown on the plan. A deadeye is taken and held point downward, while a length of thin (24 or 26 gauge) brass wire is wrapped round it, and given a few twists to tighten it. Now a large headed pin is driven into the hull about 3/8" below the channel and in line with the hole in the channel which is going to be used. The twisted part of the wire holding the deadeye is passed through this hole in the channel and over the pin (the head of the pin should have been left projecting clear of the hull), keeping the strand of the wire on either side of the shank of the pin. The free ends of the wire are twisted until they have taken a firm grip on the pin and the pin is tapped neatly home into the side of the hull and any surplus wire is cut off as close to the pin head as possible (figure 14).

When all the deadeyes have been fitted to the channels, the bowsprit is stepped and secured in place, care being taken to see that it is at the correct angle as shown on the plan, and in line with the centre line of the ship. It is a good idea to make a shallow groove along that part of the bowsprit which

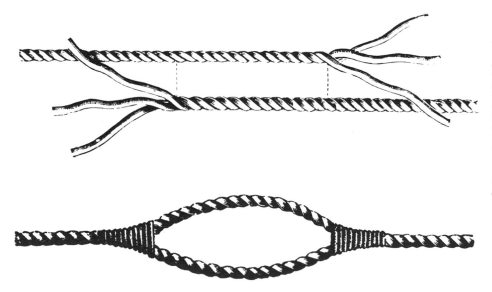

Left: To make a cut splice take two ropes and unlay both for a short distance. Place the ropes side by side with the unlaid portions facing in opposite directions and far enough apart to give an eye of the required size. Now tuck the unlaid strands under the strands of the opposite rope in the same manner as for an eye splice; after splicing both ends, cut off and smear with liquid glue, roll between the fingers. The splices may now be whipped with fine cotton.

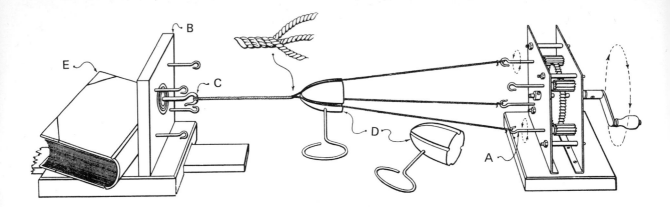

A/The 'Rope spinning jenny' should be clamped to the table. If the handle is turned in an anti-clockwise direction the four hooks will turn in a clockwise direction and produce a right hand laid rope.

B/The movable end of the set up. The central hook C is free to revolve in a ball bearing

D/The 'top'. This separates the strands of the rope and allows them to lay up evenly. When the necessary tension is reached the 'top' will start to move on its own towards the spinning machine.

E/Weights which prevent the movable end from running too quickly. The heavier the weight the harder the rope will be.

Right: *Turning mechanism of the 'Rope spinning jenny' as illustrated above made up from Meccano parts. (Picture by courtesy of John Bowen)*

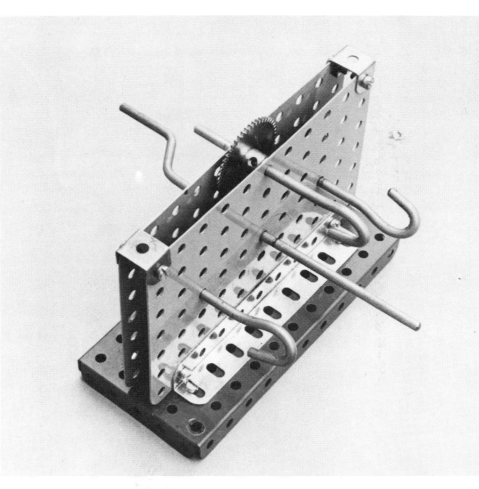

goes into the hull to prevent an airlock being created by the glue. The bowsprit is held down by the 'gammoning'. A length of fairly thick cord is taken and passed round the base of the bowsprit, down through the rectangular hole in the grating, through the rectangular hole in the centre member, and back up and over the bowsprit. Six complete turns of lashing are made and then finished off by tying the cord around itself under the bowsprit. To prevent the cord slipping backwards down the bowsprit a very fine pin must be driven in against the lowest turn.

Before 'stepping' the masts there is some more work to be done on them. With a file, flats are made on the opposite sides of the upper end of the lower masts. On the fore and main masts these extend downwards for a distance of 4.1/2". Then flats on the fore and aft faces of the masts are made over a length of 1.7/8" down from the top. Now two side cheek pieces are

Below: The port side of the half deck showing the main channel, heart shaped dead eyes and the method of securing them, the shrouds and ratlines, gunport lids and a swivel gun. On the lower corner or 'clew' of the sail are the clewline and buntline blocks

fitted to the sides of the masts (figure 15). On these rest two beams made of 1/8″ square wood, which in their turn support the circular 'top'. There are no side cheeks on the mizzen mast.

Three 'caps' are made to hold the lower and topmasts together; these are rectangles of wood 1/4″ thick for the fore and main masts and 1/8″ thick for the mizzen mast. In each are two holes, one square to fit over the squared top of the lower mast and one round to take the topmast (figure 16). The bottom, or 'heel', of the topmast must be filed square to fit into the small square hole in the circular 'top'. Two more caps for the tops of the fore and main topmasts are made to take the flagpoles. The tops of the fore and main topmasts are 'squared' to take the crosstrees and trestle-trees (figure 17).

On both the fore and main lower masts thin cord should be wound round them at intervals as shown on the plan. This is known as 'woolding' and was intended to strengthen the masts, which were usually made up of several pieces of timber. The mizzen mast does not have woolding.

The lower masts, complete with their tops but without the topmasts, are now stepped. The first item of rigging to be set up is the shrouds. These are made from fairly thick cord, which should be black or very dark brown in colour. They go over the masthead in pairs, starting with the first pair on the foremast, which are set up on the starboard (right) side looking forward. The next pair go on the port (left) side and so on alternately. On the mainmast the order is reversed and the first pair go on the port side. A fair-

Below: Two half hitches can be used to secure a rope to a spar. If it is to remain permanently the end of the rope should be secured to the standing part by a seizing.
To make a seizing take about seven turns of thread around the two parts of the rope, cross the ends of the thread and take about four turns around the original turns from top to bottom, pull tight and finish off either by tying the ends with a reef knot or by passing the ends through under the seizing.
A reef knot. Simple to make, yet if properly formed, one of the strongest of knots.

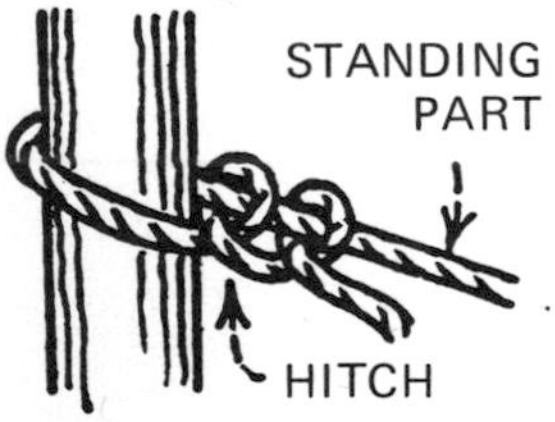

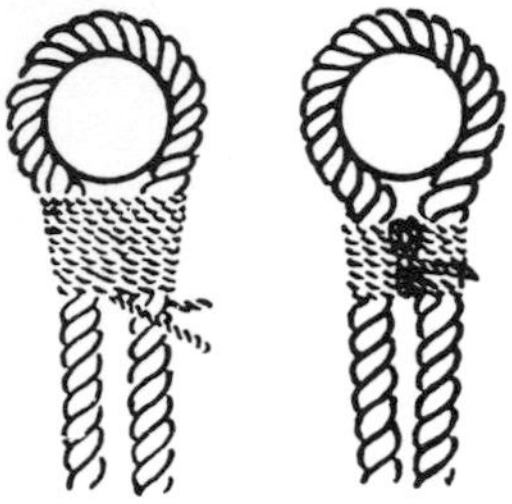

STANDING PART

FIGURE 14
FIXING LOWER DEADEYES

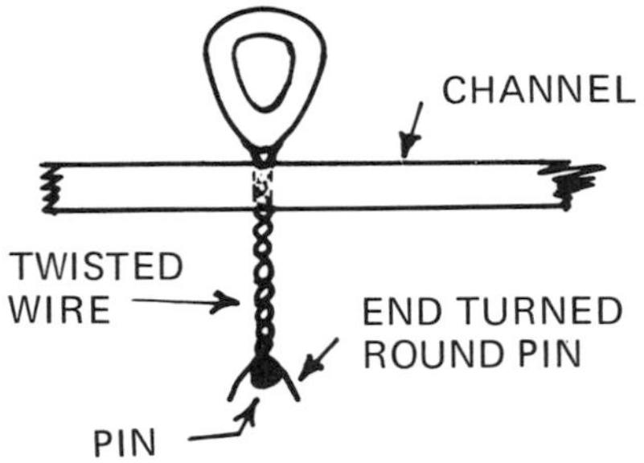

HITCH

CHANNEL

TWISTED WIRE

END TURNED ROUND PIN

PIN

FIGURE 15
MAST CHEEK PIECES

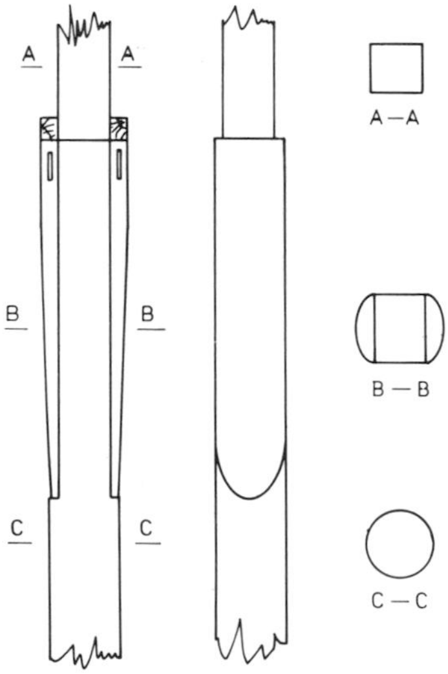

A   A

A—A

B   B

B — B

C   C

C — C

FIGURE 16
DETAIL OF CAPS

FIGURE 17
DETAIL OF UPPER CROSSTREES

FIGURE 18
BINDING SHROUDS

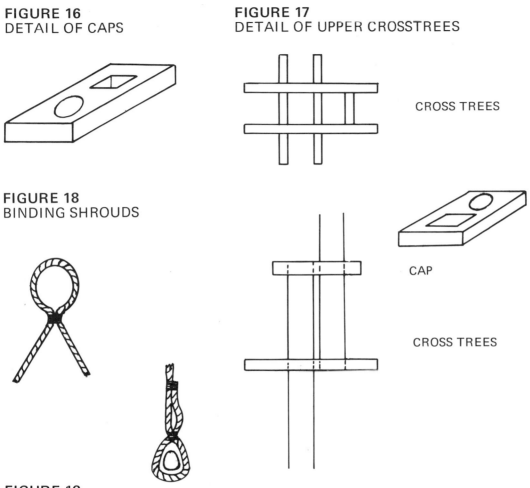

CROSS TREES

CAP

CROSS TREES

FIGURE 19
SEIZING UPPER DEADEYE

ly generous length of cord is taken, doubled, and 'seized' or bound together to leave a loop just big enough to pass over the masthead, (figure 18). The free ends are passed down through the rectangular hole in the 'top' and down to the starboard channels.

Before going further a distance gauge is made out of a piece of card in order to keep the space between the top and bottom deadeyes constant. Holding this in position, the shroud is looped round a deadeye and across itself and the loop is seized at this point with black thread (figure 19). The deadeye must be checked to make sure that it is the right way up; then the free end is carried back up the shroud for 1/2″ and two seizings are made—in other words, it is tied off with a turn or two of thread. The second shroud of the pair is made up in the same way. A piece of thin cord is passed first through the bottom deadeye and then through the top deadeye. About four turns are made in this way and the 'lanyard' as it is called, is tied off around itself. The setting up of the alternate pairs of shrouds on all three lower masts is continued. On the mizzen mast there is an odd shroud (only three a side); this should have a cut splice in the middle and one leg will then go down on each side; to avoid making a splice, it is possible to seize a loop in the middle of a length of cord and slip it over the masthead, bringing one part down on either side of the mast. When all the lower shrouds are in place and satisfactorily tightened up by the lanyards, the forestay, mainstay and mizzen stay can be fitted; they are the thickest ropes on the ship and should be of a fairly stout cord.

A start is made by measuring off the necessary length from the model and adding several inches for the loop over the top and for the deadeye at the lower end. One end is passed up through the port (left) side rectangular hole in the top, round the back of the mast and down through the starboard (right) side hole and the end is joined to the main part, either by splicing or by seizing with cotton and a touch of liquid glue; the lower ends of the stays have deadeyes 'turned in'. The forestay is connected to another deadeye which is secured to the bowsprit by a loop of cord about one third of the way from the outer end. The mainstay stops short of the foremast and

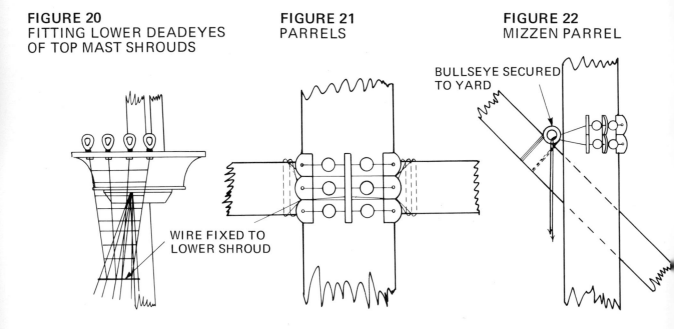

FIGURE 20
FITTING LOWER DEADEYES
OF TOP MAST SHROUDS

FIGURE 21
PARRELS

FIGURE 22
MIZZEN PARREL

BULLSEYE SECURED
TO YARD

WIRE FIXED TO
LOWER SHROUD

Left: The 'doubling' of the main topmast showing the 'cap' which connects the top of the lower mast to the bottom of the topmast. The strops of the lower deadeyes pass down through the rim of the 'top' and are secured to the lower shrouds. The mizzen topmast forestay is shown on the left of the picture; it leads to the base of the foretopmast. The fore topsail yard halliard is also visible; the hauling part starts from an eyebolt in the port channel, passes up through the block on the halliard and then down to the belaying pin rail on the starboard side gunwale.

Right: The mizzen mast showing the circular 'top' below which is the parrel holding the lateen yard to the mast; below this again is a double block lashed to the mast to lead the main topsail braces down to the pin rails on deck.

has a deadeye turned in; a length of cord is seized round the bowsprit just forward of the part where it enters the hull and at the other end of this cord is another deadeye; the two are held together by a lanyard in a similar manner to the forestay. Care should be taken to attach the forward end of the cord far enough up the bowsprit for the stay not to foul the edge of the forecastle when the lanyard is tightened up.

The topmasts should now be 'stepped' or fitted into position. The lower deadeyes of the topmast shrouds are treated in the same way as those for the lower masts except that the wire holding them is threaded through holes in the rim of the 'top' and comes down to meet the lower shrouds to which it is fastened. A short length of wire is securely tied across the lower shrouds an inch or so below the tops; the wires from the topmast lower deadeyes are then secured to it (figure 20). The pairs of shrouds for the top-masts start on the opposite side of the ship to those on the lower mast, that is, the first pair to go on the port side of the fore topmast and the first pair on the main topmast go on the starboard side. There are no deadeyes on the mizzen topmast shrouds.

The fore topmast stay goes over the crosstrees and behind the mast in a loop; the lower end has a single 'sheave' or hole rigging block seized to it, just short of the end of the bowsprit. Another block is seized to the bowsprit about an inch from the end. At the extreme outer end of the bowsprit a slightly thinner cord is fastened, which goes through the block on the fore topmast stay, down through the block on the bowsprit and back to the forecastle rail where it is belayed to the centre belaying pin. The main top-mast stay goes round the head of the topmast in a similar way to the fore topmast stay; its lower end goes through a single block seized to the lower part of the fore topmast and then down to deck where it is belayed to the rail at the after end of the forecastle. The mizzen topmast stay is seized to the mast about 1.1/2″ below the top of the pole and goes forward to the bottom of the main topmast where it is made fast by threading it down through the rectangular hole in the main top and back up the other side, and seizing it to its own part.

Now comes the rather monotonous job of 'rattling down' or tying the rat-lines across the shrouds to make the rope ladders which are so characteristic of sailing ships. It is started by ruling a series of horizontal lines on a piece of fairly stiff white card, taking the distance apart from the plan. This card can now be used as a guide by placing it behind the shrouds while tying the ratlines. The correct knot to use for this job is a clove hitch. Care must be taken not to draw the shrouds together; they should be kept straight throughout their length. It is advisable to put a touch of liquid glue on the two end knots of each ratline to prevent any possibility of them coming undone.

The running rigging comprises the halliards, lifts, braces, clewlines and leechlines (or martnets). Before starting work on these ropes it is necessary to furnish the yards with blocks as shown on the plan. The fore and main yards are held to their respective masts by 'parrels' (figure 21), which are slips of thin wood (usually about 1/16″ plywood) shaped as illustrated with three holes bored in them; four or five of these are threaded on three lengths of cord and are separated by small beads.

A start is made by taking three lengths of cord and tying them round the yard about 1/4″ off the centre; then one piece of wood is threaded on, passing one cord through each hole. Next come three beads and then another wood shape; this is continued until there are enough to go around the mast and reach the yard on the other side; finally a turn with the cords is taken around the yard and fastened off.

Below: The bowsprit showing the method of setting up the forestay and fore topmast stays.

The mizzen yard, or more correctly the lateen yard, is also held to the mast by a parrel, but this is smaller, having only two holes, and is rigged in a slightly different manner (figure 22). A length of thin cord is taken, doubled

and a bullseye (similar to a deadeye but round, not heart-shaped) is tied onto this end; the two-holed wood shapes and beads are threaded on the free ends alternately until there is enough to go around the mast and then the cord is seized. The bullseye is now attached to the yard just below mid length (see plan), and ends with the parrel just threaded up are taken and passed round the mast, through the bullseye, and down to a cleat fastened to the mast 1/2" above the deck.

The fore and main topsail yards are held to the masts in a similar manner to the lower yards but the parrels only have two holes similar to those on the mizzen yard. The spritsail yard on the bowsprit is held by a simple strap made of medium size cord.

Next come the halliards which, as their name implies, haul the yards into position on the mast. It is necessary to make three special blocks for these and the shape can be taken from the plan, although the size varies (that for the mizzen being smaller). With a fairly stout cord a couple of turns are taken around the yard slightly to one side of centre (outside the cord which fastens the parrel) and tied securely. Now the cord is taken up and passed through the hole in the cheek which supports the round 'top'. It is then taken down to the deck through the special block, back up again and forward through the hole under the 'top' on the other side. Another two turns are taken round the yard before fastening it off. The special block should have three short lengths of cord passed through and be pegged into the deck in the positions shown on the plan. The halliard should be adjusted so that the halliard block is lifted about 1" off the deck. This method applies to the three lower yards.

The spritsail yard on the bowsprit is rigged in the manner shown in the detail on the plan; a block is secured to the bowsprit 1" or so above the yard and a cord is taken round the middle of the yard, up through the block and back down to a cleat on the side of the bowsprit. The topsail yard halliards are made in two parts. First, a cord is taken round the yard and then fastened off. The other end is taken up and through a hole previously drilled in the mast about 1/2" above the yard, and then it is taken down to about two thirds of the length of the topmast and a single block is secured to the end. Now another cord is secured to a small eye made from a pin driven into the appropriate channel just abaft the aftermost deadeye. The cord is taken up and threaded through the block on the halliard and then brought down and secured to a belaying pin on the pin rail attached to the gunwale on the opposite side of the deck.

The Lifts. First single blocks are secured to the outer ends of each yard, except for the mizzen, starting with the spritsail yard; two single blocks are secured to the bowsprit about 1.1/4" from the outer end in such a way that one falls on either side of the spar. Next a fairly long piece of thin cord is taken and the middle of it is hitched to the outer end of the bowsprit. The cords now go to the blocks at the outer ends of the yard, back to the blocks on the bowsprit and then back to the belaying pin rail on the beakhead and are belayed to the two belaying pins nearest the middle. The fore yard, main yard and both topsail yards are rigged in the same manner, but in the case of the lower yards two single blocks have to be suspended under the circular tops by drilling holes in the front of the supporting platform or crosstrees and securing them there; in the case of the topsail yards two single blocks are tied under the crosstrees, one being tied on either side. All lifts come down to decks and are belayed to the belaying pin rails. The basic rule is that the higher the part operated by the rope, the further aft it is belayed.

The braces are of the type known as pendant braces; in other words, ropes are secured at each end of the yards and to each of these a single block is attached. Reference to the plan will give a clear idea of the length of these pendants. The two braces for the spritsail yard start from a common

Below: The rigging of the spritsail showing the lead of the lifts, braces, clewlines and sheets.

point on the forestay a few inches below the top; they then go down to the single pendant blocks on each yard arm, back to a double block 2″ below their starting point on the forestay and then down to another pair of single blocks, one on either side of the beakhead, and make fast to the outer belaying pins on the beakhead pin rail. The two fore braces start double in the same way on the main stay, go forward to the pendant blocks on the yard, back to a double block on the mainstay about one inch below their starting point and then to the outermost pins on the belaying pin rail on the after end of the forecastle. The main braces start at the poop rails, one on either side as shown on the plan, and go forward to the pendants on the yard, back to a single block on the poop rail and make fast to cleats on either side of the deck; these are not shown on the plan but should be attached to the gunwale just below the blocks.

The sails can be made either of parchment paper obtainable from art and craft stores, or of some soft material such as well washed poplin or old tracing linen. Rows of stitching to represent the numerous cloths or lengths of material which go to make up the sail look good, and the top edge should be neatly turned over and hemmed; the other three sides should have fine milliners' wire stitched to the edge. This makes a fair representation of the 'bolt ropes' (which are stitched round sails to strengthen them on the real thing) and allows the sails to be shaped to appear full of wind. On the fore topsail a red cross should be either painted or worked in silk. The main topsail should have the royal cypher which was a gold crown and Tudor rose in red, white and green with the letters ER in red. The sails are attached to the yards by separate short lengths of cord at intervals of about 1/2″ as shown on the plan.

If sails are fitted some more rigging is required. First the clewlines are needed. These start from the yard about 1″ out from the centre on either side and go to a block attached to the lower corner of each sail. They are then led back to another block on the yard 1/4″ nearer the centre, and so to deck where they are belayed to the next vacant pin on the belaying pin rail inside the gunwale. The 'sheets' which control the lower corners of the sails come next and, in the case of the spritsail, start as pendants attached to the lower corners of the sail. Another rope starts from an eyebolt made from a pin inserted in the gunwale just below the forecastle rail, goes forward through the pendant block and back to a hole in the gunwale about amidships, and then to a cleat attached to the gunwale as shown on the plan.

The foresail sheets start from an eyebolt (made from a pin) in the bulwarks amidships and go forward to a block on the lower corner of the foresail, then they go back to a hole in the gunwale just below the starting point and are belayed to cleats on the inside of the gunwale. The main sheets are treated in a similar way as indicated on the plan. The fore and main topsail sheets, which are attached to the corners of their respective sails, go through holes near the ends of the fore and main yards, then to blocks secured just outside the clewlines and continue on to the deck, where they are belayed to the pin rails on the gunwale. The sheets of the triangular mizzen sail start at an eyebolt in the centre of the after part of the poop deck, go up through a block on the lower corner of the sail and forward to the inner left hand (port) belaying pin on the forward end of the poop deck. At the forward end of this sail a double 'tack' (a rope fitted to haul the corner of the sail downward and forward) is attached, one part going to either side of the deck and belayed to the aftermost belaying pin on port and starboard pin rails on the half deck gunwale. The leechlines or martnets are attached to the sails by 'crowsfeet'; these are made of very thin cord attached to a slightly thicker cord. Those on the foresail lead forward to a double block on the bowsprit just forward of the forestay and back to the second belaying pin on either side of the rail at the fore end of the forecastle. Those on the mainsail go forward to a double block on the lower part of the mainstay

FIGURE 23
ANCHORS

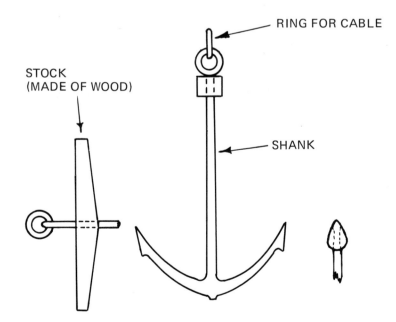

STOCK
(MADE OF WOOD)

RING FOR CABLE

SHANK

and down to the second belaying pin on either side of the rail at the after end of the forecastle. Those on the fore topsail go to a double block on the fore topmast stay, then down to another double block on the bowsprit and back to the third belaying pin on the forward forecastle rail. Those on the main topsail go to a double block on the main topmast stay and then down to the inner belaying pins on the pin rail on the after end of the forecastle.

The flags and pendants are shown full size, together with descriptions of colour. These can be made of silk and painted with watercolour paints. First a piece of material larger than the finished flag is stretched over a piece of blotting paper on a board. The outline of the design is drawn on it faintly in pencil and then painted on with a fine brush, using the colours as dry as possible consistent with working. The flag is cut out leaving a small margin on one side to wrap round the flag halliard where it will be held by a smear of glue. The flag halliards go through holes in the 'trucks' (those little round caps at the very top of the masts), and then come down to deck where they are secured to the shrouds.

Two items remain to be made: anchors and stern lanterns. The former can be cut from black plastic material such as is used for panels in radio sets. They are filed to shape as shown on the plan. The 'stock' should be shaped from wood, and a wire ring to take the anchor cable goes through a hole in the top of the shank (figure 23). The other end of the cable goes into the hawse hole in the bows of the ship. The lanterns can be built up from thin plastic card which is now available in most model shops: they should be supported on brackets made from twisted wire.

This concludes the description of the model and how it was built. Experienced craftsmen will recognise that this has been written especially for the 'first timer' and will accept it as such. Finally, it is hoped that everything has been made clear to the uninitiated and that not only will they derive pleasure and satisfaction from the work, but also that many will be converted into lifelong followers of this, one of the most satisfying of hobbies.

Bibliography. R C Anderson *The Rigging of Ships in the Days of the Spritsail Topmast* Marine Research Society, Salem, Massachusetts, United States, 1927; Guy Vercoe *English Warships in the Days of Sail* Percival Marshall & Co Ltd, 1933; Sir Westcott Abell *The Shipwright's Trade* Caravan Book Service, Jamaica 32, New York, United States, 1962; L G Carr Laughton *Old Ship Figure-heads and Sterns* Halton & Truscott Smith Ltd, London, 1925; *Sailing Ships—their history and development as illustrated by the collection of ship models in the Science Museum,* Part I Historical Notes, Part II Catalogue of Exhibits, with descriptive notes, His Majesty's Stationery Office, Part I 1931, Part II 1936; William Falconer *Universal Dictionary of the Marine* new, corrected edition, London, 1780.

model Shipwright

Advertisement

While *Modelling the Golden Hinde* provides an excellent introduction to the world of model making, the model shipwright may feel inclined to explore some of the other avenues which exist in this sphere. As an up-to-date ship modelling journal, reputed for its high standard of craftsmanship and its universal appeal, *Model Shipwright,* now in its second year, has been proved to be the vehicle through which the modeller's aspirations are enhanced.

Building on the success of our first year, each issue of Volume Two will include an extra twenty-two pages, (bringing the total to one hundred and twenty) to carry the increasing amount of material which is being submitted. The universally approved hard covers and flat opening method of binding will be retained with no increase in price.

We have been fortunate in receiving contributions from some of the world's leading authorities in this and allied spheres, but it is the model shipwrights (who now number well over three thousand) who have, through articles, letters and questions, established our journal as the international ship modelling forum. To increase still further its high standard, we shall be incorporating some full-colour plates.

Contributions from subscribers are always welcome, particularly those describing models and the way in which they were constructed, together with notes on useful jigs, tools and materials. The more drawings and photographs which accompany them the better.

Finally, we are in the process of preparing a plans service for model makers, based on authentic source material and drawn to the professional specifications expected of the journal.

Model Shipwright is published four times a year, in September, December, March and June and is of the same format as this book. If you would like to know more about *Model Shipwright* generally and the four issues of Volume Two specifically, we would be happy to send you, at no charge, a copy of our descriptive brochure.

Please send for your brochure:
Subscription Department,
Model Shipwright,
7 Nelson Road,
Greenwich,
London SE10

**A Quarterly
Journal
of Ships
and Ship models.**

Drake's circumnavigation of the world

by Richard Hakluyt (1552?-1616)

The famous voyage of sir Francis Drake into the South sea, and therehence about the globe of the whole earth, begunne Anno 1577 from THE PRINCIPAL NAVIGATIONS, VOYAGES, TRAFFIQUES & DISCOVERIES OF THE ENGLISH NATION (1598)

The 15. day of November, in the yeere of our Lord 1577. M. Francis Drake, with a fleete of five ships and barkes, and to the number of 164 men, gentlemen and sailers, departed from Plimmouth, giving out his pretended voyage for Alexandria; but the wind falling contrary, hee was forced the next morning to put into Falmouth haven in Cornewall, where such and so terrible a tempest tooke us, as few men have seene the like, and was in deed so vehement, that all our ships were like to have gone to wracke: but it pleased God to preserve us from that extremitie, and to afflict us onely for that present with these two particulars: The mast of our Admirall which was the Pellican, was cut over boord for the safegard of the ship, and the Marigold was driven ashore, and somewhat bruised: for the repairing of which damages wee returned againe to Plimmouth and having recovered those harmes, and brought the ships againe to good state, we set forth the second time from Plimmouth, and set saile the 13. day of December following.

The 25. day of the same moneth we fell with the Cape Cantin, upon the coast of Barbarie, and coasting along, the 27. day we found an Island called Mogador, lying one mile distant from the maine, betweene which Island and the maine, we found a very good and safe harbour for our ships to ride in, as also very good entrance, and voyde of any danger.

On this Island our Generall erected a pinnesse, whereof he brought out of England with him foure already framed. While these things were in doing, there came to the waters side some of the inhabitants of the countrey, shewing foorth their flags of truce, which being seene of our Generall, hee sent his ships boate to the shore, to know what they would: they being willing to come aboord, our men left there one man of our company for a pledge, and brought two of theirs aboord our ship, which by signes shewed our General, that the next day they would bring some provision, as sheepe, capons and hennes, and such like: whereupon our Generall bestowed amongst them some linnen cloth and shooes, and a javeling, which they joyfully received, and departed for that time.

The next morning they failed not to come againe to the waters side, and our Generall againe setting out our boate, one of our men leaping over rashly ashore, and offering friendly to imbrace them, they set violent hands on him, offering a dagger to his throte if hee had made any resistance, and so laying him on a horse, caried him away: so that a man cannot be too circumspect and warie of himselfe among such miscrents.

Our pinnesse being finished, wee departed from this place the 30. and last day of December, and coasting along the shore, wee did descrie, not contrary to our expectation, certaine Canters which were Spanish fishermen, to whom we gave chase and tooke three of them, and proceeding further we met with 3. Caravels and tooke them also.

The 17. day of January we arrived at Cape Blanco, where we found a ship riding at anchor, within the Cape, and but two simple Mariners in her, which ship we tooke and caried her further into the harbour, where we remained 4. dayes, and in that space our General mustered, and trayned his men on land in warlike maner, to make them fit for all occasions.

In this place we tooke of the Fishermen such necessaries as wee wanted, and they could yeeld us, and leaving heere one of our litle barkes called the Benedict, wee tooke with us one of theirs which they called Canters, being of the burden of 40. tunnes or thereabouts.

All these things being finished, wee departed this harbour the 22. of Januarie, carying along with us one of the Portugall Caravels which was bound to the Islands of Cape Verde for salt, whereof good store is made in one of those Islands.

The master or Pilot of that Caravel did advertise our Generall that upon one of those Islands called Mayo, there was great store of dryed Cabritos, which a few inhabitants there dwelling did yeerely make ready for such of the kings Ships as did there touch, beeing bound for his countrey of Brasile or elsewhere. Wee fell with this Island the 27. of January, but the Inhabitants would in no case traffique with us, being thereof forbidden by the kings Edict: yet the next day our Generall sent to view the Island, and the likelihoodes that might be there of provision of victuals, about threescore and two men under the conduct and government of Master Winter and Master Doughtie, and marching towards the chiefe place of habitation in this Island (as by the Portugall wee were informed) having travailed to the mountaines the space of three miles, and arriving there somewhat before the day breake, we arrested our selves to see day before us, which appearing, we found the inhabitants to be fled: but the place, by reason that it was manured, wee found to be more fruitfull then the other part, especially the valleys among the hils.

Here we gave our selves a litle refreshing, as by very ripe and sweete grapes, which the fruitfulnesse of the earth at that season of the yeere yeelded us: and that season being with us the depth of Winter, it may seeme strange that those fruites were then there growing: but the reason thereof is this, because they being betweene the Tropike and the Equinoctiall, the Sunne passeth twise in the yeere through their Zenith over their heads, by meanes whereof they have two Summers, & being so neere the heate of the line, they never lose the heate of the Sunne so much, but the fruites have their increase and continuance in the midst of Winter. The Island is wonderfully stored with goates and wilde hennes, and it hath salt also without labour, save only that the people gather it into heapes, which continually in great quantitie is increased upon the sands by the flowing of the sea, and the receiving heate of the Sunne kerning the same, so that of the increase thereof they keepe a continuall traffique with their neighbours.

Amongst other things we found here a kind of fruit called Cocos, which because it is not commonly knowen with us in England, I thought good to make some description of it.

The tree beareth no leaves nor branches, but at the very top the fruit groweth in clusters, hard at the top of the stemme of the tree, as big every severall fruite as a mans head: but having taken off the uttermost barke, which you shall find to bee very full of strings or sinowes, as I may terme them, you shall come to a hard shell which may holde of quantitie in liquor a pint commonly, or some a quart, and some lesse: within that shell of the thicknesse of halfe an inch good, you shall have a kinde of hard substance and very white, no lesse good and sweete then almonds: within that againe a certaine cleare liquor, which being drunke, you shall not onely finde it very delicate and sweete, but most comfortable and cordiall.

After wee had satisfied our selves with some of these fruites, wee marched further into the Island, and saw great store of Cabritos alive, which were so chased by the inhabitants, that wee could doe no good towards our provision, but they had layde out as it were to stoppe our mouthes withall, certaine olde dryed Cabritos, which being but ill, and small and few, wee made no account of.

Being returned to our ships, our Generall departed hence the 31. of this moneth, and sayled by the Island of S. Iago, but farre enough from the danger of the inhabitants, who shot and discharged at us three peeces, but they all fell short of us, and did us no harme. The Island is fayre and large, and as it seemeth, rich and fruitfull, and inhabited by the Portugals, but the mountaines and high places of the Island are sayd to be possessed by the Moores, who having bin slaves to the Portugals, to ease themselves, made escape to the desert places of the Island, where they abide with great strength.

Being before this Island, we espied two ships under sayle, to the one of which wee gave chase, and in the end boorded her with a ship-boat without resistance, which we found to be a good prize, and she yeelded unto us good store of wine: which prize our General committed to the custodie of Master Doughtie, and reteining the Pilot, sent the rest away with his Pinnesse, giving them a Butte of wine and some victuals, and their wearing clothes, and so they departed.

The same night wee came with the Island called by the Portugals, Ilha del fogo, that is, the burning Island: in the Northside whereof is a consuming fire, the matter is sayde to be of Sulphure, but notwithstanding it is like to bee a commodious Island, because the Portugals have built, and doe inhabite there.

Upon the South side thereof lyeth a most pleasant and sweete Island, the trees whereof are alwayes greene and faire to looke upon, in respect whereof they call it Ilha Brava, that is, the brave Island. From the bankes thereof into the sea doe run in many places reasonable streames of fresh waters easie to be come by, but there was no convenient roade for our ships: for such was the depth, that no ground could bee had for anchoring, and it is reported, that ground was never found in that place, so that the tops of Fogo burne not so high in the ayre, but the rootes of Brava are quenched as low in the sea.

Being departed from these Islands, we drew towards the line, where wee were becalmed the space of 3. weekes, but yet subject to divers great stormes, terrible lightnings and much thunder: but with this miserie we had the commoditie of great store of fish, as Dolphins, Bonitos, and flying fishes, whereof some fell into our shippes, wherehence they could not rise againe for want of moisture, for when their wings are drie, they cannot flie.

From the first day of our departure from the Islands of Cape Verde, wee sayled 54. dayes without sight of land, and the first land that we fell with was the coast of Brasil, which we saw the fift of April in ye height of 33. degrees towards the pole Antarctike, and being discovered at sea by the inhabitants of the countrey, they made upon the coast great fires for a sacrifice (as we learned) to the devils, about which they use conjurations, making heapes of sande and other ceremonies, that when any ship shall goe about to stay upon their coast, not onely sands may be gathered together in shoalds in every place, but also that stormes and tempests may arise, to the casting away of ships and men, whereof (as it is reported) there have bene divers experiments.

The seventh day in a mightie greate storme both of lightning, rayne and thunder, wee lost the Canter which we called the Christopher: but the eleventh day after, by our Generals great care in dispersing his ships, we found her againe, and the place where we met, our Generall called the Cape of Joy, where every ship tooke in some water. Heere we found a good temperature and sweete ayre, a very faire and pleasant countrey with an exceeding fruitfull soyle, where were great store of large and mightie Deere, but we came not to the sight of any people: but traveiling further into the countrey, we perceived the footing of people in the clay-ground, shewing that they were men of great stature. Being returned to our ships, we wayed anchor, and ranne somewhat further, and harboured our selves betweene a rocke and the maine, where by meanes of the rocke that brake the force of the sea, we rid very safe, and upon this rocke we killed for our provision certaine sea-wolves, commonly called with us Seales.

From hence we went our course to 36. degrees, and entred the great river of Plate, and ranne into 54. and 55. fadomes and a halfe of fresh water, where wee filled our water by the ships side: but our Generall finding here no good harborough, as he thought he should, bare out againe to sea the 27. of April, and in bearing out we lost sight of our Flieboate wherein master Doughtie was, but we sayling along, found a fayre and reasonable good Bay wherein were many, and the same profitable Islands, one whereof had so many Seales, as would at the least have laden all our Shippes, and the rest of the Islands are as it were laden with foules which is wonderfull to see, and they of divers sortes. It is a place very plentifull of victuals, and hath in it no want of fresh water.

Our Generall after certaine dayes of his abode in this place, being on shore in an Island, the people of the countrey shewed themselves unto him, leaping and dauncing, and entred into traffique with him, but they would not receive any thing at any mans hands, but the same must bee cast upon the ground. They are of cleane, comely, and strong bodies, swift on foote, and seeme to be very active.

The eighteenth day of May our Generall thought it needfull to have a care of such Ships as were absent, and therefore indevouring to seeke the Flieboate wherein master Doughtie was, we espied her againe the next day: and whereas certaine of our ships were sent to discover the coast and to search an harbour, the Marygold and the Canter being imployed in that businesse, came unto us and gave us understanding of a safe harbour that they had found, wherewith all our ships bare, and entred it, where we watered and made new provision of victuals, as by Seales, whereof we slew to the number of 200. or 300. in the space of an houre.

Here our Generall in the Admirall rid close aboord the Flie-boate, and tooke out of her all the provision of victuals and what els was in her, and halling her to the Lande, set fire to her, and so burnt her to save the iron worke: which being a doing, there came downe of the countrey certaine of the people naked, saving only about their waste the skinne of some beast with furre or haire on, and something also wreathed on their heads: their faces were painted with divers colours, and some of them had on their heads the similitude of hornes, every man his bow which was an ell in length, and a couple of arrowes. They were very agill people and quicke to deliver, and seemed not to be ignorant in the feates of warres, as by their order of ranging a few men, might appeare. These people would not of a long time receive any thing at our handes; yet at length our Generall being ashore, and they dauncing after their accustomed maner about him, and hee once turning his backe towards them, one leapt suddenly to him, and tooke his cap with his golde band off his head, and ran a litle distance from him and shared it with his fellow, the cap to the one, and the band to the other.

Having dispatched all our businesse in this place, wee departed and set sayle, and immediately upon our setting foorth we lost our Canter which was absent three or foure days: but when our General had her againe, he tooke out the necessaries, and so gave her over neere to the Cape of

Good hope.

The next day after being the twentieth of June, wee harboured our selves againe in a very good harborough, called by Magellan Port S. Julian, where we found a gibbet standing upon the maine, which we supposed to be the place where Magellan did execution upon some of his disobedient and rebellious company.

The two and twentieth day our Generall went ashore to the maine, and in his companie, John Thomas, and Robert Winterhie, Oliver the Master gunner, John Brewer, Thomas Hood, and Thomas Drake, and entring on land, they presently met with two or three of the countrey people, and Robert Winterhie having in his hands a bowe and arrowes, went about to make a shoote of pleasure, and in his draught his bowstring brake, which the rude Savages taking as a token of warre, began to bend the force of their bowes against our company, and drove them to their shifts very narrowly.

In this Port our Generall began to enquire diligently of the actions of M. Thomas Doughtie, and found them not to be such as he looked for, but tending rather to contention or mutinie, or some other disorder, whereby (without redresse) the successe of the voyage might greatly have bene hazarded: whereupon the company was called together and made acquainted with the particulars of the cause, which were found partly by master Doughties owne confession, and partly by the evidence of the fact, to be true: which when our Generall saw, although his private affection to M. Doughtie (as he then in the presence of us all sacredly protested) was great, yet the care he had of the state of the voyage, of the expectation of her Majestie, and of the honour of his countrey did more touch him, (as indeede it ought) then the private respect of one man: so that the cause being thoroughly heard, and all things done in good order as neere as might be to the course of our lawes in England, it was concluded that M. Doughtie should receive punishment according to the qualitie of the offence: and he seeing no remedie but patience for himselfe, desired before his death to receive the Communion, which he did at the hands of M. Fletcher our Minister, and our Generall himselfe accompanied him in that holy action: which being done, and the place of execution made ready, hee having embraced our Generall and taken his leave of ali the companie, with prayer for the Queenes majestie and our realme, in quiet sort laid his head to the blocke, where he ended his life. This being done, our Generall made divers speaches to the whole company, perswading us to unitie, obedience, love, and regard of our voyage; and for the better confirmation thereof, willed every man the next Sunday following to prepare himselfe to receive the Communion, as Christian brethren and friends ought to doe, which was done in very reverent sort, and so with good contentment every man went about his businesse.

The 17. day of August we departed the port of S. Julian. & the 20. day we

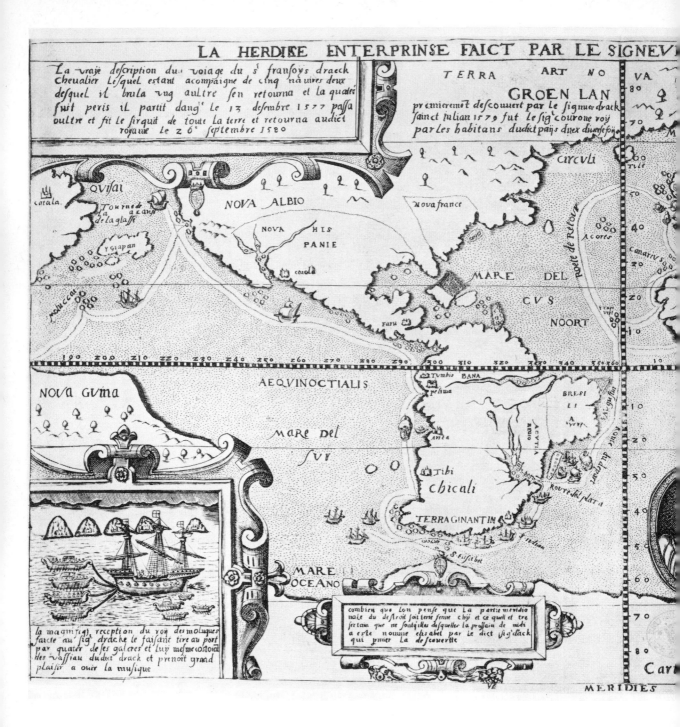

La magnifiq. reception du roy des moluques
faicte au sig. dracke le faisant tire au port
par quater de ses galeres et luy mesme contoia
des vassiau du dict drack et prenoit grand
plaisir a ouir la musique

72

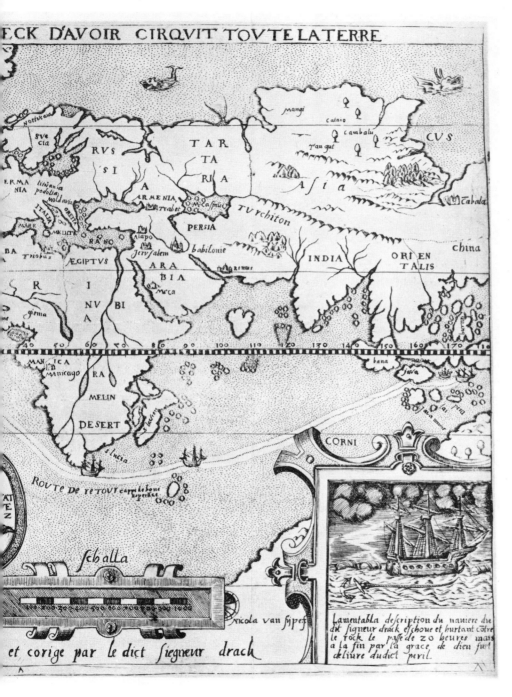

ECK D'AVOIR CIRQVIT TOVTE LA TERRE

mangi

Cainio

Cambalu

CVS

Tanqut

Notiveau

SVE
cia

RVS
SI
A

TAR
TA
RI
A

Asia

Tabala

ERMA
NIA

*litvania
podolia
moldavia*

ARMENIA
M.Caspiu
Trabet

TVRchiton

ITALIA
MARE
MEDITE

RA
NO

Aiapo

PERSIA

babilonie

Ierusalem

INDIA

ORIEN
TALIS

china

BA

Triobus

MEUTE

AEGIPTVS

ARA
BIA

Mecca

R.Remus

R
I
NV BI
A

Roma

DESERT

S.lucia

CORNI

bana

java

ROVTE DE RETOVR *capitlebone Esperance*

schalla

nicola van sipesf

Lamentabla description du naviere du
dit signeur draick eschoue et hurtant contre
le rock le passe de 20 heures mais
a la fin par la grace de dieu fust
deliure dudict peril

et corige par le dict sieigneur drach

Arguably the earliest map which shows Drake's route. The decoration, style and cartographical inaccuracy—the stumpy shape given to South America—all support a date before 1600. In addition, Cavendish's voyage (1586–8), which is almost always shown on maps of the period, is not marked. The portrait of Drake is clearly very early and it seems unlikely that this would have been chosen if the more famous portrait of 1586 had been in existence.

There is some evidence to suggest that it was made in Antwerp; the watermark on the paper reveals the name of Jean Nivelle, a well-known paper maker from Troyes whose merchandise was frequently used by the Antwerp printers.

Of particular interest on the map are the insets in the lower corners, illustrating the two outstanding episodes of the voyage: the reception given to the 'Golden Hinde' by the Sultan of Ternate, and the perilous position of the vessel when she ran upon the reef off Celebes.

Finally, the many mistakes on the map, for example, the words CORNI and CUS which are probably remnants of an earlier map, standing respectively for TROPICUS CAPRICORNI and TROPICUS CANCRI—again point to an early date and suggest that the map was carelessly rushed into circulation to capitalize upon Drake's feat which would doubtless have been the major topic of conversation.

fell with the streight or freat of Magellan going into the South sea, at the Cape or headland whereof we found the bodie of a dead man, whose flesh was cleane consumed.

The 21. day we entred The streight, which we found to have many turnings, and as it were shuttings up, as if there were no passage at all, by meanes whereof we had the wind often against us, so that some of the fleete recovering a Cape or point of land, others should be forced to turne backe againe, and come to an anchor where they could.

In this streight there be many faire harbors, with store of fresh water, but yet they lacke their best commoditie: for the water is there of such depth, that no man shal find ground to anchor in, except it bee in some narrow river or corner, or betweene some rocks, so that if any extreme blasts or contrary winds do come (whereunto the place is much subject) it carieth with it no small danger.

The land on both sides is very huge & mountainous, the lower mountains whereof, although they be monstrous and wonderfull to looke upon for their height, yet there are others which in height exceede them in a strange maner, reaching themselves above their fellowes so high, that betweene them did appeare three regions of cloudes.

These mountaines are covered with snow: at both the Southerly and Easterly partes of the streight there are Islands, among which the sea hath his indraught into the streights, even as it hath in the maine entrance of the freat.

This streight is extreme cold, with frost and snow continually: the trees seeme to stoope with the burden of the weather, and yet are greene continually, and many good and sweete herbes doe very plentifully grow and increase under them.

The bredth of the streight is in some place a league, in some other places 2. leagues, and three leagues, and in some other 4. leagues, but the narrowest place hath a league over.

The 24. of August we arrived at an Island, in the streights, where we found great store of foule which could not flie, of the bignesse of geese, whereof we killed in lesse then one day 3000. and victualled our selves throughly therewith.

The 6. day of September we entred the South sea at the Cape or head shore.

The seventh day wee were driven by a great storme from the entring into the South sea two hundred leagues and odde in longitude, and one degree to the Southward of the Streight: in which height, and so many leagues to the Westward, the fifteenth day of September fell out the Eclipse of the Moone at the houre of sixe of the clocke at night: but neither did the Eclipticall conflict of the Moone impayre our state, nor her clearing againe amend us a whit, but the accustomed Eclipse of the Sea continued in his force, wee being darkened more then the Moone seven fold.

From the Bay (which we called The Bay of severing of friends) wee were driven backe to the Southward of the streights in 57. degrees and a terce: in which height we came to an anker among the Islands, having there fresh and very good water, with herbes of singular vertue. Not farre from hence we entred another Bay, where wee found people both men and women in their Canoas, naked, and ranging from one Island to another to seeke their meat, who entered traffique with us for such things as they had.

We returning hence Northward againe, found the 3. of October three Islands, in one of which was such plentie of birdes as is scant credible to report.

The 8. day of October we lost sight of one of our Consorts wherein M. Winter was, who as then we supposed was put by a storme into the streights againe, which at our returne home wee found to be true, and he not perished, as some of our company feared.

Thus being come into the height of The streights againe, we ran, supposing the coast of Chili to lie as the generall Maps have described it, namely Northwest, which we found to lie and trend to the Northeast and East-wards, whereby it appeareth that this part of Chili hath not bene truely hitherto discovered, or at the least not truely reported for the space of 12. degrees at the least, being set downe either of purpose to deceive, or of ignorant conjecture.

We continuing our course, fell the 29. of November with an Island called la Mocha, where we cast anchor, and our Generall hoysing out our boate, went with ten of our company to shore, where wee found people, whom the cruell and extreme dealings of the Spaniards have forced for their owne safetie and libertie to flee from the maine, and to fortifie themselves in this Island. We being on land, the people came downe to us to the water side with shew of great courtesie, bringing to us potatoes, rootes, and two very fat sheepe, which our Generall received and gave them other things for them, and had promise to have water there: but the next day repayring againe to the shore, and sending two men aland with barrels to fill water, the people taking them for Spaniards (to whom they use to shew no favour if they take them) layde violent hands on them, and as we thinke, slew them.

Our Generall seeing this, stayed here no longer, but wayed anchor, and set sayle towards the coast of Chili, and drawing towards it, we mette neere to the shore an Indian in a Canoa, who thinking us to have bene Spaniards, came to us and tolde us, that at a place called S. Iago, there was a great Spanish ship laden from the kingdome of Peru: for which good newes our Generall gave him divers trifles, whereof he was glad, and went along with us and brought us to the place, which is called the port of Valparizo.

When we came thither, we found indeede the ship riding at anker, having in her eight Spaniards and three Negros, who thinking us to have bene

Spaniards and their friends, welcommed us with a drumme, and made ready a Bottija of wine of Chili to drinke to us: but as soone as we were entred, one of our company called Thomas Moone began to lay about him, and strooke one of the Spanyards, and sayd unto him, Abaxo Perro, that is in English, Goe downe dogge. One of these Spaniards seeing persons of that quality in those seas, all to crossed, and blessed himselfe: but to be short, wee stowed them under hatches all save one Spaniard, who suddenly and desperately leapt over boord into the sea, and swamme ashore to the towne of S. Iago, to give them warning of our arrivall.

They of the towne being not above 9. housholds, presently fled away and abandoned the towne. Our generall manned his boate, and the Spanish ships boate, and went to the Towne, and being come to it, we rifled it, and came to a small chappell which wee entred, and found therein a silver chalice, two cruets, and one altar-cloth, the spoyle whereof our Generall gave to M. Fletcher his minister.

We found also in this towne a warehouse stored with wine of Chili, and many boords of Cedar-wood, all which wine we brought away with us, and certaine of the boords to burne for fire-wood: and so being come aboord, wee departed the Haven, having first set all the Spaniards on land, saving one John Griego a Greeke borne, whom our Generall caried with him for his Pilot to bring him into the haven of Lima.

When we were at sea, our Generall rifled the ship, and found in her good store of the wine of Chili, and 25000. pezoes of very pure and fine gold of Baldivia, amounting in value to 37000. ducats of Spanish money, and above. So going on our course, wee arrived next at a place called Coquimbo, where our Generall sent 14. of his men on land to fetch water: but they were espied by the Spaniards, who came with 300. horsemen and 200 footemen, and slewe one of our men with a piece, the rest came aboord in safetie, and the Spaniards departed: wee went on shore againe, and buried our man, and the Spaniards came downe againe with a flag of truce, but we set sayle and would not trust them.

From hence we went to a certaine port called Tarapaza, where being landed, we found by the Sea side a Spaniard lying asleepe, who had laying by him 13 barres of silver, which weighed 4000. ducats Spanish; we tooke the silver, and left the man.

Not farre from hence going on land for fresh water, we met with a Spaniard and an Indian boy driving 8. Llamas or sheepe of Peru which are as big as asses; every of which sheepe had on his backe 2. bags of leather, each bagge conteining 50. li. weight of fine silver: so that bringing both the sheepe and their burthen to the ships, we found in all the bags 800. weight of silver.

Here hence we sailed to a place called Arica, and being entred the port, we found there three small barkes which we rifled, and found in one of them

76

57 wedges of silver, each of them weighing about 20 pound weight, and every of these wedges were of the fashion and bignesse of a brickbat. In all these 3. barkes we found not one person: for they mistrusting no strangers, were all gone aland to the Towne, which consisteth of about twentie houses, which we would have ransacked if our company had bene better and more in number. But our Generall contented with the spoyle of the ships, left the Towne and put off againe to sea and set sayle for Lima, and by the way met with a small barke, which he boorded, and found in her good store of linnen cloth, whereof taking some quantitie, he let her goe.

To Lima we came the 13. day of February, and being entred the haven, we found there about twelve sayle of ships lying fast moored at an anker, having all their sayles caried on shore: for the masters and marchants were here most secure, having never bene assaulted by enemies, and at this time feared the approch of none such as we were. Our generall rifled these ships, and found in one of them a chest full of royals of plate, and good store of silkes and linnen cloth, and tooke the chest into his owne ship, and good store of the silkes and linnen. In which ship hee had newes of another ship called the Cacafuego which was gone toward Paita, and that the same shippe was laden with treasure: whereupon we staied no longer here, but cutting all the cables of the shippes in the haven, we let them drive whither they would, either to sea or to the shore, and with all speede we followed the Cacafuego toward Paita, thinking there to have found her: but before wee arrived there, she was gone from thence towards Panama, whom our Generall still pursued, and by the way met with a barke laden with ropes and tackle for ships, which hee boorded and searched, and found in her 80. li. weight of golde, and a crucifixe of gold with goodly great Emerauds set in it which he tooke, and some of the cordage also for his owne ship.

From hence we departed, still following the Cacafuego, and our Generall promised our company, that whosoever could first descrie her, should have his chaine of gold for his good newes. It fortuned that John Drake going up into the top, descried her about three of the clocke, and about sixe of the clocke we came to her and boorded her, and shotte at her three peeces of ordinance, and strake downe her Misen, and being entered, we found in her great riches, as jewels and precious stones, thirteene chests full of royals of plate, foure score pound weight of golde, and sixe and twentie tunne of silver. The place where we tooke this prize, was called Cape de San Francisco, about 150. leagues from Panama.

The Pilots name of this Shippe was Francisco, and amongst other plate that our Generall found in this ship, he found two very faire guilt bowles of silver, which were the Pilots: to whom our Generall sayd: Senior Pilot, you have here two silver cups, but I must needes have one of them: which the Pilot because hee could not otherwise chuse, yeelded unto, and gave the other to the steward of our Generals ships.

When this Pilot departed from us, his boy sayde thus unto our Generall: Captaine, our ship shall be called no more the Cacafuego, but the Cacaplata, and your shippe shall bee called the Cacafuego: which pretie speach of the Pilots boy ministred matter of laughter to us, both then and long after.

When our Generall had done what hee would with this Cacafuego, hee cast her off, and wee went on our course still towards the West, and not long after met with a ship laden with linnen cloth and fine China-dishes of white earth, and great store of China-silks, of all which things wee tooke as we listed.

The owner himselfe of this ship was in her, who was a Spanish Gentleman, from whom our Generall tooke a Fawlcon of golde, with a great Emeraud in the breast thereof, and the Pilot of the ship he tooke also with him, and so cast the ship off.

This Pilot brought us to the haven of Guatulco, the towne whereof, as he told us, had but 17. Spaniards in it. Assoone as we were entred this haven, wee landed, and went presently to the towne, and to the Towne-house, where we found a Judge sitting in judgement, being associate with three other officers, upon three Negros that had conspired the burning of the Towne: both which Judges & prisoners we tooke, and brought them a ship-boord, and caused the chiefe Judge to write his letter to the Towne, to command all the Townesmen to avoid, that we might safely water there. Which being done, and they departed, we ransaked the Towne, and in one house we found a pot of the quantitie of a bushell, full of reals of plate, which we brought to our ship.

And here one Thomas Moone one of our company, tooke a Spanish Gentleman as hee was flying out of the towne, and searching him, he found a chaine of golde about him, and other jewels, which he tooke, and so let him goe.

At this place our General among other Spaniards, set ashore his Portugall Pilote, which hee tooke at the Islands of Cape Verde, out of a ship of S. Mary port of Portugall: and having set them ashore, we departed hence, and sailed to the Island of Canno, where our Generall landed, and brought to shore his owne ship, and discharged her, mended, and graved her, and furnished our ship with water and wood sufficiently.

And while wee were here, we espied a shippe, and set saile after her, and tooke her, and found in her two Pilots, and a Spanish Governour, going for the Islands of the Philippinas: wee searched the shippe, and tooke some of her marchandizes, and so let her goe. Our Generall at this place and time, thinking himselfe both in respect of his private injuries received from the Spaniards, as also of their contempts and indignities offered to our countrey and Prince in generall, sufficiently satisfied, and revenged: and supposing that her Majestie at his returne would rest contented with this service, purposed to continue no longer upon the Spanish coasts, but began to consider and to consult of the best way for his Countrey.

He thought it not good to returne by the Streights, for two speciall causes: the one, lest the Spaniards should there waite, and attend for him in great number and strength, whose hands, hee being left but one ship, could not possibly escape. The other cause was the dangerous situation of the mouth of the streights in the South sea, where continuall stormes reigning and blustering, as he found by experience, besides the shoalds and sands upon the coast, he thought it not a good course to adventure that way: he resolved therefore to avoyde these hazards, to goe forward to the Islandes of the Malucos, and therehence to saile the course of the Portugals by the Cape of Buena Esperanza.

Upon this resolution, hee beganne to thinke of his best way to the Malucos, and finding himselfe where he now was becalmed, he saw that of necessitie hee must be forced to take a Spanish course, namely to sayle somewhat Northerly to get a winde. Wee therefore set saile, and sayled 600. leagues at the least for a good winde, and thus much we sailed from the 16. of April, till the 3. of June.

The 5. day of June, being in 43. degrees towards the pole Arctike, we found the ayre so colde, that our men being grievously pinched with the same, complained of the extremitie thereof, and the further we went, the more the colde increased upon us. Whereupon we thought it best for that time to seeke the land, and did so, finding it not mountainous, but low plaine land, till wee came within 38. degrees towards the line. In which height it pleased God to send us into a faire and good Baye, with a good winde to enter the same.

In this Baye wee anchored, and the people of the Countrey having their houses close by the waters side, shewed themselves unto us, and sent a present to our Generall.

When they came unto us, they greatly wondred at the things that wee brought, but our Generall (according to his naturall and accustomed humanitie) courteously intreated them, and liberally bestowed on them necessary things to cover their nakednesse, whereupon they supposed us to be gods, and would not be perswaded to the contrary: the presents which they sent to our Generall, were feathers, and calles of net-worke.

Their houses are digged round about with earth, and have from the uttermost brimmes of the circle, clifts of wood set upon them, joyning close together at the toppe like a spire steeple, which by reason of that closenesse are very warme.

Their beds is the ground with rushes strowed on it, and lying about the house, have the fire in the midst. The men go naked, the women take bulrushes, and kembe them after the manner of hempe, and thereof make their loose garments, which being knit about their middles, hang down about their hippes, having also about their shoulders a skinne of Deere, with the haire upon it. These women are very obedient and serviceable to their husbands.

After they were departed from us, they came and visited us the second time, and brought with them feathers and bags of Tabacco for presents: And when they came to the top of the hill (at the bottome whereof we had pitched our tents) they staied themselves: where one appointed for speaker wearied himselfe with making a long oration, which done, they left their bowes upon the hill, and came downe with their presents.

In the meane time the women remaining on the hill, tormented themselves lamentably, tearing their flesh from their cheekes, whereby we perceived that they were about a sacrifice. In the meane time our Generall with his company went to prayer, and to reading of the Scriptures, at which exercise they were attentive, & seemed greatly to be affected with it: but when they were come unto us, they restored againe unto us those things which before we bestowed upon them.

The newes of our being there being spread through the Countrey, the people that inhabited round about came downe, and amongst them the King himselfe, a man of a goodly stature, & comely personage, with many other tall and warlike men: before whose comming were sent two Ambassadors to our Generall, to signifie that their King was comming, in doing of which message, their speach was continued about halfe an houre. This ended, they by signes requested our Generall to send some thing by their hand to their king, as a token that his comming might be in peace: wherein our Generall having satisfied them, they returned with glad tidings to their King, who marched to us with a princely majestie, the people crying continually after their manner, and as they drew neere unto us, so did they strive to behave themselves in their actions with comelinesse.

In the fore-front was a man of a goodly personage, who bare the scepter or mace before the King, whereupon hanged two crownes, a lesse and a bigger, with three chaines of a marveilous length: the crownes were made of knit worke wrought artificially with fethers of divers colours: the chaines were made of a bonie substance, and few be the persons among them that are admitted to weare them: and of that number also the persons are stinted, as some ten, some 12. &c. Next unto him which bare the scepter, was the King himselfe, with his Guard about his person, clad with Conie skins, & other skins: after them followed the naked common sort of people, every one having his face painted, some with white, some with blacke, and other colours, & having in their hands one thing or another for a present, not so much as their children, but they also brought their presents.

In the meane time our Generall gathered his men together, and marched within his fenced place, making against their approching a very warre-like shew. They being trooped together in their order, and a generall salutation being made, there was presently a generall silence. Then he that bare the scepter before the King, being informed by another, whom they assigned to that office, with a manly and loftie voyce proclaymed that which the other spake to him in secrete, continuing halfe an houre: which ended, and a generall Amen as it were given, the King with the whole number of men and women (the children excepted) came downe without any weapon, who descending to the foote of the hill, set themselves in order.

In comming towards our bulwarks and tents, the scepter-bearer began a song, observing his measures in a daunce, and that with a stately countenance, whom the King with his Guarde, and every degree of persons following, did in like maner sing and daunce, saving onely the women, which daunced & kept silence. The General permitted them to enter within our bulwarke, where they continued their song and daunce a reasonable time. When they had satisfied themselves, they made signes to our General to sit downe, to whom the King, and divers others made several orations, or rather supplications, that hee would take their province and kingdome into his hand, and become their King, making signes that they would resigne unto him their right and title of the whole land, and become his subjects. In which, to perswade us the better, the King and the rest, with one consent, and with great reverence, joyfully singing a song, did set the crowne upon his head, inriched his necke with all their chaines, and offred unto him many other things, honouring him by the name of Hioh, adding thereunto as it seemed, a signe of triumph: which thing our Generall thought not meete to reject, because he knew not what honour and profit it might be to our Countery. Wherefore in the name, and to the use of her Majestie he tooke the scepter, crowne, and dignitie of the said Countery into his hands, wishing that the riches & treasure thereof might so conveniently be transported to the inriching of her kingdom at home, as it aboundeth in ye same.

The common sorte of people leaving the King and his Guarde with our Generall, scattered themselves together with their sacrifices among our people, taking a diligent viewe of every person: and such as pleased their fancie, (which were the yongest) they inclosing them about offred their sacrifices unto them with lamentable weeping, scratching, and tearing the flesh from their faces with their nailes, whereof issued abundance of blood. But wee used signes to them of disliking this, and stayed their hands from force, and directed them upwards to the living God, whom onely they ought to worship. They shewed unto us their wounds, and craved helpe of them at our hands, whereupon we gave them lotions, plaisters and oyntments, agreeing to the state of their griefes, beseeching God to cure their diseases. Every third day they brought their sacrifices unto us, until they understood our meaning, that we had no pleasure in them: yet they could not be long absent from us, but dayly frequented our company to the houre of our departure, which departure seemed so greevous unto them, that their joy was turned into sorow. They intreated us, that being absent we would remember them, and by stealth provided a sacrifice, which we misliked.

Our necessarie businesse being ended, our General with his company travailed up into the Countrey to their villages, where we found herdes of Deere by 1000. in a company, being most large, and fat of body.

We found the whole Countrey to bee a warren of a strange kinde of Connies, their bodies in bignesse as be the Barbary Connies, their heads as the heads of ours, the feete of a Want, and the taile of a Rat being of great length: under her chinne is on either side a bag, into the which she gathereth her meate, when she hath filled her bellie abroad. The people eate their bodies, and make great accompt of their skinnes, for their Kings coate was made of them.

Our Generall called this Countrey Nova Albion, and that for two causes: the one in respect of the white bankes and cliffes, which lie towards the sea: and the other, because it might have some affinitie with our Countrey in name, which sometime was so called.

There is no part of earth heere to bee taken up, wherein there is not some shew of gold or silver.

At our departure hence our Generall set up a monument of our being there, as also of her Majesties right and title to the same, namely a plate, nailed upon a faire great poste, whereupon was ingraven her Majesties name, the day and yeere of our arrivall there, with the free giving up of the province and people into her Majesties hands, together with her highnesse picture and armes, in a peece of six pence of current English money under the plate, whereunder was also written the name of our Generall.

It seemeth that the Spaniards hitherto had never bene in this part of the countrey, neither did ever discover the land by many degrees, to the Southwards of this place.

After we had set saile from hence, wee continued without sight of land till the 13. day of October following, which day in the morning wee fell with certaine Islands 8. degrees to the Northward of the line, from which Islands came a great number of Canoas, having in some of them 4. in some 6. and in some also 14. men, bringing with them cocos, and other fruites. Their Canoas were hollow within, and cut with great arte and cunning, being very smooth within and without, and bearing a glasse as if it were a horne daintily burnished, having a prowe, and a sterne of one sort, yeelding inward circle-wise, being of a great height, and full of certaine white shels for a braverie, and on each side of them lie out two peeces of timber about a yard and a halfe long, more or lesse, according to the smalnesse, or bignesse of the boate.

This people have the nether part of their eares cut into a round circle, hanging downe very lowe upon their cheekes, whereon they hang things of reasonable weight. The nailes of their hands are an ynche long, their teeth are as blacke as pitch, and they renew them often, by eating of an herbe with a kinde of powder, which they alwayes carrie about them in a cane for the same purpose.

Leaving this Island the night after we fell with it, the 18. of October, we lighted upon divers others, some whereof made a great shew of Inhabitants.

Wee continued our course by the Islands of Tagulada, Zelon, and Zewarra, being friends to the Portugals, the first whereof hath growing in it great store of Cinnamom.

The 14. of November we fell with the Islands of Maluco, which day at night (having directed our course to runne with Tydore) in coasting along the Island of Mutyr, belonging to the King of Ternate, his Deputie or Vice-king seeing us at sea, came with his Canoa to us without all feare, and came aboord, and after some conference with our Generall, willed him in any wise to runne in with Ternate, and not with Tydore, assuring him that the King would bee glad of his comming, and would be ready to doe what he would require, for which purpose he himselfe would that night be with the King, and tell him the newes, with whom if he once dealt, hee should finde that as he was a King, so his word should stand: adding further, that if he went to Tydore before he came to Ternate, the King would have nothing to doe with us, because hee held the Portugall as his enemie: whereupon our General resolved to runne with Ternate, where the next morning early we came to anchor, at which time our Generall sent a messenger to the king with a velvet cloke for a present, and token of his comming to be in peace, and that he required nothing but traffique and exchange of marchandize, whereof he had good store, in such things as he wanted.

In the meane time the Vice-king had bene with the king according to his promise, signifying unto him what good things he might receive from us by traffique: whereby the King was mooved with great liking towards us, and sent to our Generall with speciall message, that hee should have what things he needed, and would require with peace and friendship, and moreover that hee would yeeld himselfe, and the right of his Island to bee at the pleasure and commandement of so famous a Prince as we served. In token whereof he sent to our Generall a signet, and within short time after came in his owne person, with boates, and Canoas to our ship, to bring her into a better and safer roade then she was in at present.

In the meane time, our Generals messenger beeing come to the Court, was met by certaine noble personages with great solemnitie, and brought to the King, at whose hands hee was most friendly and graciously intertained.

The King purposing to come to our ship, sent before 4. great and large Canoas, in every one whereof were certaine of his greatest states that were about him, attired in white lawne of cloth of Calicut, having over their heads from the one ende of the Canoa to the other, a covering of thinne perfumed mats, borne up with a frame made of reedes for the same use, under which every one did sit in his order according to his dignitie, to keepe him from the heate of the Sunne, divers of whom beeing of good age and gravitie, did make an ancient and fatherly shew. There were also divers yong and comely men attired in white, as were the others: the rest were souldiers, which stood in comely order round about on both sides, without whom sate the rowers in certaine galleries, which being three on a side all along the Canoas, did lie off from the side thereof three or foure yardes, one being orderly builded lower then another, in every of which galleries were the number of 4. score rowers.

These Canoas were furnished with warlike munition, every man for the most part having his sword and target, with his dagger, beside other weapons, as launces, calivers, darts, bowes and arrowes: also every Canoa had a small cast base mounted at the least one full yarde upon a stocke set upright.

Thus comming neere our shippe, in order they rowed about us, one after another, and passing by, did their homage with great solemnitie, the great personages beginning with great gravitie and fatherly countenances, signifying that ye king had sent them to conduct our ship into a better roade.

Soone after the King himselfe repaired, accompanied with 6. grave and ancient persons, who did their obeisance with marveilous humilitie. The king was a man of tall stature, and seemed to be much delighted with the sound of our musicke, to whom as also to his nobilitie, our Generall gave presents, wherewith they were passing well contented.

At length the King craved leave of our Generall to depart, promising the next day to come aboord, and in the meane time to send us such victuals, as were necessarie for our provision: so that the same night we received of them meale, which they call Sagu, made of the tops of certaine trees, tasting in the mouth like sowre curds, but melteth like sugar, whereof they make certaine cakes, which may be kept the space of ten yeeres, and yet then good to be eaten. We had of them store of rice, hennes, unperfect and liquid sugar, sugar canes, and a fruite which they call Figo, with store of cloves.

The King having promised to come aboord, brake his promise, but sent his brother to make his excuse, and to intreate our Generall to come on shoare, offring himselfe pawne aboord for his safe returne. Whereunto our Generall consented not, upon mislike conceived of the breach of his promise, the whole company also utterly refusing it. But to satisfie him, our General sent certaine of his Gentlemen to the Court, to accompany the King's brother, reserving the Vice-king for their safe returne. They were received of another brother of the kings, and other states, and were conducted with great honour to the Castle. The place that they were brought unto, was a large and faire house, where were at the least 1000. persons assembled.

The King being yet absent, there sate in their places 60. grave personages, all which were said to be of the kings Counsel. There were besides 4. grave persons, apparelled all in red, downe to the ground, and attired on their heads like the Turkes, and these were said to be Romanes, and Ligiers there to keepe continual traffike with the people of Ternate. There were also 2. Turks Ligiers in this place, and one Italian. The king at last came in guarded with 12. launces covered over with a rich canopy, with embossed gold. Our men accompanied with one of their Captaines called Moro, rising to meete him, he graciously did welcome, and intertaine them. He was attired after the manner of the Countrey, but more sumptuously then the rest. From his waste downe to the ground, was all cloth of golde, and the same very rich: his legges were bare, but on his feete were a pair of shooes, made of Cordovan skinne. In the attire of his head were finely wreathed hooped rings of gold, and about his necke he had a chaine of perfect golde, the linkes whereof were great, and one folde double. On his fingers hee had sixe very faire jewels, and sitting in his chaire of estate, at his right hand stood a page with a fanne in his hand, breathing and gathering the ayre to the King. The fanne was in length two foote, and in bredth one foote, set with 8. saphyres, richly imbrodered, and knit to a staffe 3. foote in length, by the which the Page did hold, and moove it. Our Gentlemen having delivered their message, and received order accordingly, were licensed to depart, being safely conducted backe againe by one of the kings Counsell.

This Island is the chiefest of all the Islands of Maluco, and the King hereof is King of 70. Islands besides. The king with his people are Moores in religion, observing certaine new Moones, with fastings: during which fasts, they neither eat nor drinke in the day, but in the night.

After that our Gentlemen were returned, and that we had heere by the favour of the king received all necessary things that the place could yeeld us: our General considering the great distance, and how farre he was yet off from his Countrey, thought it not best here to linger the time any longer, but waying his anchors, set out of the Island, and sayled to a certaine litle Island to the Southwards of Celebes, where we graved our ship, and continued there in that and other businesses 26. dayes. This Island is throughly growen with wood of a large and high growth, very straight and without boughes, save onely in the head or top, whose leaves are not much differing from our broome in England. Amongst these trees night by night, through the whole land, did shew themselves an infinite swarme of fiery wormes flying in the ayre, whose bodies beeing no bigger then our common English flies, make such a shew and light, as if every twigge or tree had bene a burning candle. In this place breedeth also wonderfull store of Bats, as bigge as hennes: of Crayfishes also heere wanted no plentie, and they of exceeding bignesse, one whereof was sufficient for 4. hungry stomacks at a dinner, beeing also very good, and restoring meate, whereof we had experience:

and they digge themselves holes in the earth like Conies.

When wee had ended our businesse here, we waied, and set saile to runne for the Malucos: but having at that time a bad winde, and being amongst the Islands, with much difficultie wee recovered to the Northward of the Island of Celebes, where by reason of contrary winds not able to continue our course to runne Westwards, we were inforced to alter the same to the Southward againe, finding that course also to be very hard and dangerous for us, by reason of infinite shoalds which lie off, and among the Islands: whereof wee had too much triall to the hazard and danger of our shippe and lives. For of all other dayes upon the 9. of Januarie, in the yeere 1579. wee ranne suddenly upon a rocke, where we stucke fast from 8. of the clocke at night til 4. of the clocke in the afternoone the next day, being indeede out of all hope to escape the danger: but our Generall as hee had alwayes hitherto shewed himselfe couragious, and of a good confidence in the mercie and protection of God: so now he continued in the same, and lest he should seeme to perish wilfully, both he, and we did our best indevour to save our selves, which it pleased God so to blesse, that in the ende we cleared our selves most happily of the danger.

We lighted our ship upon the rockes of 3. tunne of cloves, 8 peeces of ordinance, and certaine meale and beanes: and then the winde (as it were in a moment by the speciall grace of God) changing from the starreboord to the larboord of the ship, we hoised our sailes, and the happy gale drove our ship off the rocke into the sea againe, to the no litle comfort of all our hearts, for which we gave God such prayse and thanks, as so great a benefite required.

The 8. of Februarie following, wee fell with the fruitfull Island of Barateve, having in the meane time suffered many dangers by windes and shoalds. The people of this Island are comely in body and stature, and of a civill behaviour, just in dealing, and courteous to strangers, whereof we had the experience sundry wayes, they being most glad of our presence, and very ready to releeve our wants in those things which their Countrey did yeelde. The men goe naked, saving their heads and privities, every man having something or other hanging at their eares. Their women are covered from the middle downe to the foote, wearing a great number of bracelets upon their armes, for some had 8. upon each arme, being made some of bone, some of horne, and some of brasse, the lightest whereof by our estimation waied two ounces apeece.

With this people linnen-cloth is good marchandize, and of good request, whereof they make rols for their heads, and girdles to weare about them.

Their Island is both rich and fruitfull: rich in golde, silver, copper, and sulphur, wherein they seeme skilfull and expert, not onely to trie the same, but in working it also artificially into any forme and fashion that pleaseth them.

86

Their fruits be divers and plentiful, as nutmegs, ginger, long pepper, lemmons, cucumbers, cocos, figu, sagu, with divers other sorts: and among all the rest, wee had one fruite, in bignesse, forme, and huske, like a Bay berry, hard of substance, and pleasant of taste, which being sodden, becommeth soft, and is a most good and wholsome victuall, whereof we tooke reasonable store, as we did also of the other fruits and spices: so that to confesse a trueth, since the time that we first set out of our owne Countrey of England, we happened upon no place (Ternate onely excepted) wherein we found more comforts and better meanes of refreshing.

At our departure from Barateve, we set our course for Java major, where arriving, we found great courtesie, and honourable entertainment. This Island is governed by 5. Kings, whom they call Rajah: as Rajah Donaw, and Rajah Mang Bange, and Rajah Cabuccapollo, which live as having one spirite, and one minde.

Of these five we had foure a shipboord at once, and two or three often. They are wonderfully delighted in coloured clothes, as red and greene: their upper parts of their bodies are naked, save their heads, whereupon they weare a Turkish roll, as do the Maluccians: from the middle downward they weare a pintado of silke, trailing upon the ground, in colour as they best like.

The Maluccians hate that their women should bee seene of strangers: but these offer them of high courtesie, yea the kings themselves.

The people are of goodly stature, and warlike, well provided of swords and targets, with daggers, all being of their owne worke, and most artificially done, both in tempering their mettall, as also in the forme, whereof we bought reasonable store.

They have an house in every village for their common assembly: every day they meete twise, men, women, and children, bringing with them such victuals as they thinke good, some fruites, some rice boiled, some hennes roasted, some sagu, having a table made 3. foote from the ground, whereon they set their meate, that every person sitting at the table may eate, one rejoycing in the company of another.

They boile their rice in an earthen pot, made in forme of a sugar loafe, being ful of holes, as our pots which we water our gardens withall, and it is open at the great ende, wherein they put their rice drie, without any moisture. In the meane time they have ready another great earthen pot, set fast in a fornace, boiling full of water, whereinto they put their pot with rice, by such measure, that they swelling become soft at the first, and by their swelling stopping the holes of the pot, admit no more water to enter, but the more they are boiled, the harder and more firme substance they become, so that in the end they are a firme & good bread, of the which with oyle, butter, sugar, and other spices, they make divers sorts of meates very pleasant of taste, and nourishing to nature.

The French pocks is here very common to all, and they helpe themselves, sitting naked from ten to two in the Sunne, whereby the venemous humour is drawen out. Not long before our departure, they tolde us, that not farre off there were such great Ships as ours, wishing us to beware: upon this our Captaine would stay no longer.

From Java Major we sailed for the cape of Good Hope, which was the first land we fell withall: neither did we touch with it, or any other land, untill we came to Sierra Leona, upon the coast of Guinea: notwithstanding we ranne hard aboord the Cape, finding the report of the Portugals to be most false, who affirme, that it is the most dangerous Cape of the world, never without intolerable stormes and present danger to travailers, which come neere the same.

This Cape is a most stately thing, and the fairest Cape we saw in the whole circumference of the earth, and we passed by it the 18. of June.

From thence we continued our course to Sierra Leona, on the coast of Guinea, where we arrived the 22. of July, and found necessarie provisions, great store of Elephants, Oisters upon trees of one kind, spawning and increasing infinitely, the Oister suffering no budde to grow. We departed thence the 24. day.

We arrived in England the third of November 1580. being the third yeere of our departure.

The brass plaque discovered at Drake's Bay in 1936, near the probable landing place of Drake and his crew. A transcription of the text appears at the beginning of the next page.

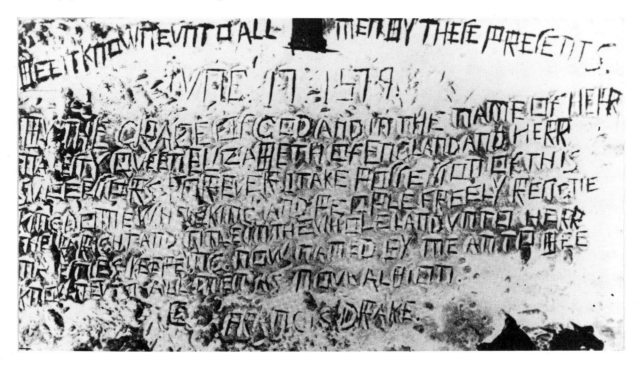

88

The Appledore replica

by Stephen Morrison

Bee it knowne vnto all men by these presents, by the grace of God and in the name of Herr Majesty Qveen Elizabeth of England and Herr svccessors forcver, I take possession of this kingdome whose king and people freely resigne their right and title in the whole land vnto Herr Majesties keepeing, now named by me an to bee knowne vnto all men as Nova Albion'. The brass plate on which this inscription was carved was nailed to a tree in the San Francisco Bay area on 17 June 1579. The name below it was that of Francis Drake.

Although the claim to 'the whole land' was never subsequently pressed with any great seriousness by the English court, and leaving aside the fact that the brass plate documents the arrival of the first European on the American Continent[1] the event proved to be of long-lasting significance. Despite the fact that it was the Spaniards finally who colonized the area, the name of the captain of the *Golden Hinde* has consistently exercised a compelling influence on the imaginations of the residents of San Francisco and the surrounding area, so much so that two enterprising Californians embarked on a project to create a tangible manifestation of this four-hundred year old 'link'.

In the face of overwhelming problems of finance, the lack of historical records, the paucity of accurate design information and the stringency of present-day maritime regulations, Albert Elledge, a San Francisco business man and Art Blum, president of a major public relations firm in the United States, set out to create the first full-scale, historically authentic sailing replica of the *Golden Hinde* and to sail her across the Atlantic from Plymouth to berth her at Fisherman's Wharf, San Francisco as a permanent memorial to Drake's visit.

Of the problems just mentioned, perhaps the most difficult which marine architect Christian Norgaard had to overcome was the total absence of any authentic document relating to the actual construction of the vessel. Some measure of this formidable stumbling block can be gauged from the tentative remarks above (Pp 13—14) which are solely concerned with one aspect of the problem—the dimensions and tonnage.

Another aspect, that of pictorial representation, is almost equally fruitless. At least two sources, however, do provide some visual material although their very nature seems to discount the possibility of their being in any way accurate and trustworthy. A general idea of the *Golden Hinde* can be assessed from a minute ship, engraved on a gold band round the cup, formed of a coconut shell, presented by Drake to Queen Elizabeth. Much the same type of representation is to be found on the only other definite source, Judocus Hondius' *Charte of the World* of about 1595.

Christian Norgaard, who undertook the task of creating designs for a ship that almost everyone had heard of but no-one had described with any

1 with the exception of the Vikings.

Left: The replica of 'Golden Hinde' entering the water. Note the full shape and lines of the hull, the bluff bow—and the absence of the customary timber assembly of the fore poppet or bow cradle. The hawse holes are clearly visible, and the channels and lower deadeyes for the foremast shrouds are in place. Note the run of the planking to the beakhead. (Picture by courtesy of Douglas Allen)

Left to right: Oswald Bennett (77) is one of the few remaining skilled riggers versed in the intricacies of rigging a ship of this kind. He is here seen serving a rope which has already been parcelled, that is, bound with tarred canvas or hessian. Note the shape of the special serving mallet, and the way the tarred line is taken round the head and the handle so that it will always be taut as the rigger passes the mallet round and round the rope. (Picture by courtesy of Douglas Allen)
The adze, seen here in use on preparing some timber, is one of the shipwright's principal tools, and one which has changed little for hundreds of years.
Metal spikes (or rose head patent nails) have been used to secure the planking. Although many traditional methods have been used in building this replica of the 'Golden Hinde,' full use has been made of modern tools – such as the electric drill in the foreground. (Picture by courtesy of A C Littlejohns)

accuracy, spent three years collecting and studying every scrap of the available information before he felt confident enough to prepare plans which would faithfully represent what the sixteenth century shipwright, with his crude system of ratios, had conceived with his eye.

The final product, in historical terms, shows the *Golden Hinde* to have been a typical mid-sixteenth century warship during the transition from the earlier carrack to the later galleon, showing the influence of the Venetian style of shipbuilding widespread at the time. The replica, with a length of over 100' and weighing a little over 100 tons, carries three masts and some 4,150 square feet of sail.

That the choice of building the *Golden Hinde* should fall on the shipyard of J Hinks & Sons of Appledore was no fortuitous decision; indeed, its aptness cannot be doubted. It is fitting that the county of England which provided Francis Drake four hundred years ago should now create a replica of his most famous vessel, destined to rest at Fisherman's Wharf as a constant reminder of the ties between Devon and Marin County, San Francisco.

In addition, the wisdom of selecting this yard becomes more apparent because it was probably the only yard in Europe capable of using the traditional techniques of the sixteenth century required in the building of this ship. Previously, it had constructed a replica of the seventeenth century ketch *The Nonesuch* for the Hudson Bay Company of Canada, and the small team of shipwrights involved had acquired invaluable experience of the special techniques required in building this historic vessel.

This gives a good idea of the stem and the bow frames. The shipwright in the foreground is securing a plank in place with clamps preparatory to final fitting. (Picture by courtesy of Douglas Allen)

The insistence on authenticity demanded an equal attention to the interior of Drake's vessel. Cannons, sail, small arms and armour, leather buckets and graplins, portraits and furniture—all the items which would have been carried on the original ship had to be carefully researched and re-created from sixteenth century models.

There are eighteen cannon on the *Golden Hinde,* fourteen sakers and four slightly smaller falcons. They were designed by Cliff Matthews, probably Britain's only authentic cannon maker, who was also responsible for the cannon on *The Nonesuch.* The actual casting was carried out under his supervision at the foundry of Vosper Thorneycroft in Portsmouth. Once fitted to the gun carriages, the cannon, each supplied with full loading and priming gear, will be as complete as those carried on the original vessel.

Woodcarving was fairly limited on ships of the sixteenth century, in contrast with later vessels, and on the *Golden Hinde* is confined to the figurehead of a gilded hind's head, a carved lion for the top of the rudderpost and the knightheads. The work was carried out by Jack Whitehead and Norman Gaches, two internationally-famous marine woodcarvers who also used their talents on *The Nonesuch.*

The beautifully carved Tudor furniture that will be carried on the *Golden Hinde* replica is a joint product of the arts of these three craftsmen. Prepared and made by Cliff Matthews, all the items of furniture have been elaborately carved to original Tudor designs, and the best English oak has been used throughout.

Other equally traditional and rare crafts have been employed in the rigging and sail-making. The rigging has been prepared by Joe and Oswald Bennett, two brothers from Appledore who are among the very last riggers to be brought up in the trade. Using a variety of traditional tools, some of them virtually museum pieces, the two brothers, who crewed some of the last

Left: This view gives a very good idea of the changing shape of the hull from midships aft. The two shipwrights in the foreground are preparing the keel to receive the next pair of half frames. (Picture by courtesy of A C Littlejohns)
Right: The hull planking has been completed; note the run of the planking to the beakhead. (Picture by courtesy of Douglas Allen)

Four stages in stepping the mast. (Picture by courtesy of Tony Freeman).

sailing ships out of Appledore, came out of retirement to work on the standing and running rigging.

The sails, which are woven from flax and carefully sewn by hand, as in the sixteenth century, were made by W C Lucas Ltd of Portsmouth, who have been making sails since 1887 and are one of only two or three firms in Britain still making sails in the traditional way.

The small arms, helmets, armour and muskets which the *Golden Hinde* will carry have been made by Calcraft Products Ltd of Gunnislake in Cornwall, a firm which specializes in authentic period reproductions and which was specially commissioned to produce the artefacts for the interior of the vessel.

The culmination of the planning and the hard work arrived at about eight o'clock in the evening of 5 April when the Countess of Devon launched the *Golden Hinde.* Several weeks were then spent in fitting her out to prepare her for her sea-trials in late May and early June which, at the time of writing, are nearing completion. Before setting out on her one and only crossing of the Atlantic, the *Golden Hinde* will be berthed at Plymouth between 16 June and 23 June at Mayflower steps, and at London, from 1 July until 9 September at Tower Pier. Californians apart, these are the only times dur-which this superb replica will be on view to the general public.

Her captain is Adrian Small, a forty-three year old experienced seaman who lives in Brixham, Devon. Captain Small, who has been sailing in square-rigged sailing ships since he was sixteen, was second mate in the *Mayflower* replica and skippered the *Nonesuch* on her voyages around the South Coast of England.

Her First Mate is Mr St J H Daniel, a member of the staff of the National Maritime Museum, who has been given leave of absence by the Trustees to sail with Captain Small. During the deep sea voyage, he intends to carry out a research project for the Museum using instruments similar to those carried by Drake.

On the voyage to San Francisco, estimated to take 142 days, Captain Small will carry a crew of between fifteen and twenty, less than a quarter of the number carried by Drake, most of whom were mariners and 'gentlemen'.

When the Golden Hinde sets sail from Plymouth at the end of September on her voyage to San Francisco, she will be more than just a tribute to the energy and the enterprise of Drake and his fellow mariners. Equally, the replica pays tribute to the unique imagination and initiative of her California owners and to the rare skills of the many craftsmen from Devon and other parts of Britain whose work can be seen in every line and curve of her structure and on every facet of the artefacts contained in her. At her final mooring in San Francisco, the *Golden Hinde* will be a constant and colourful reminder of the creative skill of her many makers, and a worthy memorial to the historic links between the Bay and the County of Devon.